Contemporary Illustrations for Preachers, Teachers, and Writers

Also by Craig Brian Larson

Illustrations for Preaching & Teaching
Preaching That Connects
Hang in There . . . To the Better End

Contemporary Illustrations for Preachers, Teachers, and Writers

Craig Brian Larson

Baker Books

A Division of Baker Book House Co
Grand Rapids, Michigan 49516

Published by Baker Books
a division of Baker Book House Company
P.O. Box 6287, Grand Rapids, MI 49516-6287

Second printing, December 1997

Printed in the United States of America

Library of Congress Cataloging-in-Publication Data

Larson, Craig Brian.
    Contemporary illustrations for preachers, teachers, and writers / Craig Brian Larson.
        p. cm.
    Includes bibliographical references and indexes.
    ISBN 0-8010-9020-2 (cloth)
       1. Homiletical illustrations. 2. Storytelling—Religious aspects—Christianity. I. Title.
    BV4225.2.L37 1996
    252'.08—dc20   96-6790

For information about academic books, resources for Christian leaders, and all new releases available from Baker Book House, visit our web site: http://www.bakerbooks.com

Contents

Introduction

Leadership Journal once asked Ravi Zacharias how to reach people in our postmodern society. "One of the important roles of the preacher is to be a connector," said Zacharias.

"What has helped me in making the connection," he explained, "is to see a sermon as incorporating three components: the argument (or proclamation), the illustration, and the application. The Scriptures provide the truth; the arts, poetry, literature, or other current events provide the illustrations; and the application should go right to daily living. This approach helps connect ideas with concrete reality."

I found it fascinating that someone as strong in abstract thinking as Zacharias would say illustrations are key to connecting. Pastors in the trenches know he's right.

I also found it fascinating that in the same issue of *Leadership*, John Ortberg, with tongue only partly in cheek, took to task books of "canned" illustrations because some of their illustrations aren't true. He makes a good point. The problem isn't illustrations organized in books; the problem is illustrations that are mythical or general or too old to feel relevant. Illustrations that connect best with today's listeners are contemporary and credible.

Contemporary. Nearly all the illustrations in this book are taken from magazines and newspapers of the 1980s and '90s.

Credible. These illustrations use people's names (when the story does not reflect negatively on them), dates, and places. I usually document the source for each illustration as a brief reference within the illustration and in detail in the notes (quoting these sources will cause credibility to rise).

The book includes several other features:

Expanded alternative subjects. Since illustrations can be
adapted for use with many subjects, I've listed alternative
subjects beneath each illustration, which are also referenced in the subject index (the most important tool for
the usefulness of this book).

Scripture index. Each illustration is also indexed under
familiar preaching Scriptures.

May the Holy Spirit use these stories and illustrations to
convey his truth to this generation.

Abundant Life 1

Many men would love to lead the life of Sean Connery. Tall, handsome, and dashing, Connery played the glamorous part of 007 in six James Bond movies. Connery travels the world to shoot movies in places as exotic as equatorial Africa or the Orient. In addition to acting, Connery works as the executive producer of films, a position of considerable power.

Yet when asked in an interview why, at age sixty-two, he continues to act, Connery gave a surprising reply: "Because I get the opportunity to be somebody better and more interesting than I am."

Many people feel like Connery. Their lives aren't all that they could be. They aren't as good as they should be. Something is missing that even glamorous acting roles cannot fulfill.

Only Christ makes a person's life what it can be, should be, and must be.

Christlikeness, Salvation
John 10:10

Date used _____ Place _____

Accountability 2

On February 26, 1995, Barings, the oldest bank in Britain, announced it was seeking bankruptcy protection after losing nearly one billion dollars in a stock gamble. At the time Barings went under, the bank held assets for Queen Elizabeth, some $100 million according to *Time* magazine.

In late 1994, the chief trader at Barings's Singapore office began betting big on Japan's Nikkei market. Then disaster struck. An earthquake hit Kobe, Japan, and on January 23, 1995, the Nikkei plunged more than one thousand points.

Barings Bank lost big money. But instead of cutting his losses, Barings's Singapore trader doubled his investment, apparently hoping that the Nikkei would rebound. It didn't. As the Nikkei continued to plummet, Barings's London office put up nearly $900 million to support its falling position on the Singapore investments. Finally Barings ran out of capital and declared bankruptcy.

How could one twenty-eight-year-old trader in Singapore lose nearly a billion dollars and ruin a 233-year-old British bank? According to *Time*, the problem was lack of supervision.

London allowed [the Singapore trader] to take control of both the trading desk and the backroom settlement operation in Singapore. It is a mix that can be—and in this case was—toxic. . . . For a trader to keep his own books is like a schoolboy getting to grade his own tests; the temptation to cheat can be overwhelming, particularly if the stakes are high enough.

Without accountability, temptation becomes all the more tempting. Accountability protects us from ourselves.

Deception, Integrity, Management, Risk, Temptation
Prov. 4:26; 10:9; 14:8; 2 Cor. 8:21; Eph. 5:21

Date used _____ Place _____

In *World Christian,* John Huffman describes one unforgettable moment with his daughter. He had been away from home for several weeks on an overseas missions trip. When his airplane landed, he could hardly wait to see his wife and four children, but he and the other passengers were detained in customs for two hours. Finally the customs officials allowed Huffman to proceed to the lobby, where hundreds of people were anxiously waiting for family and friends. Huffman writes:

There was such a press of bodies, I knew I would not be able to pick my children out until I walked up the ramp, past security, and got out into the open. But my three-year-old daughter, who had managed to squeeze her way to the front of the crowd, began screaming at the top of her lungs, "Daddy! Daddy! That's my daddy!" She must have shouted that at least five times, when suddenly she broke free from the crowd, and bolted past the security guards, still yelling, "Daddy! Daddy! That's my daddy!" She literally flew into my arms and began kissing and hugging me. What a welcome! I have never felt so loved and acknowledged in my life. It was a wonderful, fulfilling moment that even today brings a warm and happy feeling.

That, says John Huffman, is what God feels like when we acknowledge him in worship.

Children, God the Father, Worship
John 4:23–24

Date used _____ Place _____

Admonishment 4

On Monday, February 6, 1995, according to the *Chicago Tribune*, a Detroit bus driver finished his shift on the Route 21 bus and headed for the terminal. But somehow he took a wrong turn. He didn't arrive at the terminal at the scheduled time of 7:19 P.M., and a short time later his supervisors started looking for him. Meanwhile the driver's wife called the terminal and reported her husband might be disoriented from medication he was taking.

For six hours, the forty-foot city bus and its driver could not be found. Finally the state police found the bus and driver—two hundred miles northwest of Detroit. The bus was motoring slowly down a rural two-lane road, weaving slightly from side to side. The police pulled the bus over, and the driver said he was lost.

A police news release later stated, "The driver had no idea where he was and agreed he had made a wrong turn somewhere. Apparently this had not occurred to him during the four hours he drove without finding the bus depot."

Unless we confront those who have taken a wrong turn in life, they may never regain their orientation.

Backsliding, Confrontation, Confusion,
Intervention, Lostness, Shepherding
Gal. 6:1–2; James 5:19–20

Date used _____ Place _____

Adoption 5

In *Reader's Digest,* a contributor told of an Aunt Ruby and Uncle Arnie who had adopted a baby boy after five years of trying unsuccessfully to conceive. To their surprise, a short time after the adoption, Aunt Ruby discovered she was pregnant, and she later gave birth to a boy.

One day when the two boys were eight and nine years old, the teller of the story was visiting Aunt Ruby, and a woman in the neighborhood came to visit.

Observing the children at play, the woman asked, "Which boy is yours, Ruby?"

"Both of them," Aunt Ruby replied.

The caller persisted. "But I mean, which one is adopted?"

Aunt Ruby did not hesitate. In her finest hour, she looked straight at her guest and replied, "I've forgotten."

When we are adopted as God's children, we quickly come to cherish our heavenly Father's forgetfulness. For he chooses to forget our sins, to forget our wayward past, and to give us the full rights of sons or daughters. He treats us as if we had never sinned.

Forgetting sin, Forgiveness, God the Father, Salvation
Rom. 8:1–17; Eph. 1:5; Heb. 8:12

Date used _____ Place _____

Former President Richard Nixon gave and took a lot of advice. In his presidential campaign against John F. Kennedy, however, he paid the price for not listening to the wise counsel of Dwight Eisenhower. Otto Friedrich in *Time* magazine writes:

> Eisenhower and others warned Nixon not to accept Kennedy's challenge to a televised debate—Nixon was the Vice President, after all, and far better known than the junior Senator from Massachusetts—but Nixon took pride in his long experience as a debater. He also ignored advice to rest up for the debate and went on campaigning strenuously until the last minute. So, what a record 80 million Americans saw on their TV screens was a devastating contrast. Kennedy looked fresh, tanned, vibrant; Nixon looked unshaven, baggy-eyed, surly. The era of the politics of TV imagery had begun, and the debates were a major victory for Kennedy.

Kennedy, of course, went on to win the presidency with 50.4 percent of the popular vote and Nixon a hairwidth behind at 49.6 percent. Most analysts say if it hadn't been for the debacle at the televised debate, Nixon would have won the election.

Counsel, Decisions, Pride, Teachability
Prov. 15:22

Date used _____ Place _____

In *Wishful Thinking,* Frederick Buechner writes:

Of the seven deadly sins, anger is possibly the most fun. To lick your wounds, to smack your lips over grievances long past, to roll over your tongue the prospect of bitter confrontations still to come, to savor to the last toothsome morsel both the pain you are given and the pain you are giving back—in many ways it is a feast fit for a king. The chief drawback is that what you are wolfing down is yourself. The skeleton at the feast is you.

Forgiveness, Grievances, Revenge
1 Cor. 13:5; 1 Tim. 2:8

Date used _____ Place _____

Eric Zorn writes in the *Chicago Tribune* of a tragic accident that shows the terrible power of anger.

According to Zorn, a man and woman were driving a van in the far left lane of Chicago's Northwest Tollway in April 1994. In back were their two children. A white Cadillac driven by an ex-convict suddenly pulled up behind them, tailgating mere inches from their bumper. The man driving the van slowed down. The Cadillac driver pulled into the right lane, passed the van, and then swerved suddenly back in front of the van, so suddenly that the van driver felt he had to swerve to avoid a collision.

The white Cadillac sped away.

The van driver accelerated and gave chase. He eventually pulled alongside the white Cadillac and reportedly began yelling and screaming. According to a witness, the two men gestured angrily at each other.

The driver of the Cadillac then pulled a handgun and fired at the van. The bullet entered the side of the van and hit the baby girl, entering under her left ear and exiting above her right ear. The little girl lived, but she is blind in one eye, half-blind in the other, partially deaf, and suffers severe mental and physical disabilities.

The man who fired the bullet is in jail.

The parents of the little girl must now live with the terrible pain of regret.

Anger usually escalates—often in tragic, tragic ways.

Forgiveness, Regret, Self-control, Temper
Matt. 5:21–22, 38–42; Eph. 4:26–31; James 1:19–20

Date used _____ Place _____

Anger is hazardous to your health.

In a study conducted by the Gallup Organization and reported in 1994, Philadelphia ranked first among U.S. cities on what was called the "hostility index." The hostility index was based on a nine-question scale that asked people how they felt about such things as loud rock music, supermarket checkout lines, and traffic jams. Other cities on the hostility top five were New York, Cleveland, Chicago, and Detroit. At the bottom of the hostility index were Des Moines, Minneapolis, Denver, Seattle, and Honolulu.

Medical experts looking at the results felt it was no coincidence that the cities that rated high on the hostility index also had higher death rates. Commenting on the study, Dr. Redford Williams of Duke University Medical School said, "Anger kills. There is a strong correlation between hostility and death rates. The angrier people are and the more cynical they are, the shorter their life span."

Emotions, Health, Hostility
Rom. 8:5–7; Gal. 5:19–23

Date used _____ Place _____

Anxiety

How can we quiet our fears and worries?

The answer is something like the new technology being developed to quiet noise in the workplace. Several companies now market headphones that emit what is called antinoise.

"The principle behind all antinoise devices is the same," writes Philip Elmer-Dewitt in *Time*. "Noise is basically a pressure wave traveling through the air. Antinoise is the mirror image of that wave, an equal and opposite vibration exactly 180 degrees out of phase with the noise to be blocked. When noise and antinoise collide, they interact with what is called destructive interference, canceling each other out."

Airport baggage handlers can now wear headphones equipped with a tiny microphone that "samples sound waves at the wearer's ear, processes them through special circuitry, and broadcasts countertones that cancel the offending sounds in midair. Result: silence, or something close to it."

In the same way, we can cancel worries and fears with the antinoise of God's truth.

Devotional life, Faith, Fear, Peace, Promises, Trust, Truth
Eph. 6:16–17

Date used _____ Place _____

Appearance

Jeff Pierce was the 1994 captain of the Chevrolet-L.A. Sheriff professional cycling team and a top competitor. In 1987 he won one stage of the Tour de France. But in 1994, according to *USA Today,* he accepted an interesting and potentially dangerous assignment. To prepare for an article he planned to write for a magazine called *Bicycle Guide,* Pierce worked for a month as a bike messenger in downtown New York. On the streets for eleven hours a day, he dodged taxis and buses, sometimes reaching a speed of thirty-nine miles an hour on his custom-made, $2,500 racing bike. Was he worried about this expensive bike being stolen as he dashed into buildings to deliver his packages?

You bet he was. To thwart thieves, Pierce wrapped duct tape around the frame of his bike and spray-painted it black. His bike looked like a piece of junk, and his plan worked. No one touched it.

We cannot always judge value by appearance.

Character, Externals, Judgment, Ministry
1 Sam. 16:7; John 7:24; 1 Cor. 1:18–31

Date used _____ Place _____

Frenchman Michel Lotito has an iron gut.

For some reason Lotito likes to eat metal. In the past twenty-five years, says writer Rosie Mestel, Lotito has eaten eleven bicycles, seven shopping carts, a metal coffin, a cash register, a washing machine, a television, and 660 feet of fine chain.

Lotito says it wasn't easy eating his first bicycle: "I started with the metal and moved on to the tires," he recalls. "It was really difficult to stay that extra day to finish off the rubber. Metal's tasteless, but rubber is horrible." Now Lotito swallows pieces of tire and frame together.

But none of that can compare with his biggest meal: a Cessna. That's right, Lotito has eaten an entire light airplane, 2,500 pounds of aluminum, steel, vinyl, Plexiglas, and rubber.

With a meal like that he cuts the metal into pieces about the size of his fingernail and consumes about two pounds a day.

Most people would agree that Michel Lotito has an unhealthy appetite.

When we first come to Christ, we have appetites just as unhealthy. New believers need to change their appetites from what is not food at all to what is true food for the soul.

Devotional life, Entertainment, Thoughts
Rom. 16:18; Phil. 4:8; 1 Peter 2:1–3

Date used _____ Place _____

Arguing

According to the *Chicago Tribune*, one husband and wife from London, England, had more than their share of arguments. One day in 1994 they argued so sharply that the wife got in their car and ran over him. The husband, who was fifty-five years old, lived, but he suffered forty-five leg fractures and a skull fracture. He was hospitalized for five months, and his wife was thrown into jail for grievous bodily harm.

Then the husband did a remarkable—and some might say dubious—thing. He asked the court to set her free. "I can't live without her," said the man, now wheelchair-bound. In response to his request, the Newcastle court suspended his wife's sentence.

The husband told the *Daily Telegraph* (London), "We are back together and happy," but he added, "She's very argumentative."

Although this man displayed some remarkable forgiveness, that marriage is clearly not made in heaven. An argumentative attitude is stubborn, ugly, and destructive.

Fights, Forgiveness, Marriage, Peacemakers
Matt. 5:9; Phil. 2:14; 2 Tim. 2:23–24

Date used _____ Place _____

You may want to have a fire extinguisher handy when you eat horseradish made by Ellen LaBombard of Fairmont, New York. LaBombard horseradish comes in four varieties: Regular Hot, X Hot, XXX Hot, and Too Darn Hot. One of the ingredients in her hottest horseradish used to be a secret ingredient: allyl isothiocyanate. That spice is no longer a secret.

According to the *Chicago Tribune*, on February 13, 1995, Ellen accidentally spilled a one-and-a-half-quart bottle of the spice in her basement. She plugged in a fan to try to air out the room, but the overwhelming vapors forced her out. She called 911, but when the Fairmont firefighters came, they too were overwhelmed—and they were wearing masks! So they called in none other than the Onondaga County Hazardous Materials Unit! They evidently were able to clean up the spill.

The fire chief later explained to the media that the liquid spice is dangerous if inhaled in large amounts.

Even the finest spice can be overwhelming when we get too much of it. In the same way, the doctrines and disciplines of the Christian life must be kept in balance.

Church, Doctrine, Extremes, Knowledge, Preaching, Spirituality, Zeal
Eccles. 7:16–18; Phil. 1:9–11

Date used _____ Place _____

Blindness

In 1995 *Jane's International Defense Review* reported that Norinco of China was offering to export a weapon that used laser beams to damage the eyes of enemies. The weapon is called the ZM–87 portable laser "disturber."

According to the *Chicago Tribune,* "Jane's said the company states 'one of its major applications' is 'to injure or dizzy' the eyes of an enemy combatant with high-power laser pulses, and 'especially anybody who is sighting and firing . . . [by means of] an optical instrument, so as to cause him to lose combat ability or result in suppression of his observation and sighting operation.'"

The ZM–87 is effective to a range of two miles.

Blinding a soldier renders him worthless for battle. Satan knows that, and so he too has weapons to blind the eyes.

Lies, Satan, Spiritual warfare
2 Cor. 4:4

Date used _____ Place _____

Most dictionaries list names of famous people. The editors must make difficult decisions about whom to include and whom to exclude. *Webster's New World Dictionary,* for example, includes Audrey Hepburn but leaves out Spencer Tracy. It lists Bing Crosby, not Bob Hope; Willie Mays, not Mickey Mantle.

Executive editor Michael Agnes explains that names make the cut based on their frequency of use and their usefulness to the reader, but contemporary entertainers are not included.

For that reason, Elton John and Michael Jackson aren't in the dictionary, but Marilyn Monroe and Elvis Presley are.

There is another book far more important than the dictionary. In this book also, some names are included and others excluded. It is called the Book of Life. Only those listed in its pages will enter the glory of heaven and eternal life. The sole criterion for those included: sincere faith in Jesus Christ.

Name, Salvation
Rev. 20:11–15

Date used _____ Place _____

Brokenness

In his book *Broken in the Right Place*, Alan Nelson writes:

My boys are at the age when they like gliders, the cheap, balsa wood airplanes. The thin, light wood is prestamped so that you punch out the airplane and attach the wings to the fuselage. The balsa wood is supposed to break off at the grooves. Sometimes it does not. Occasionally you splinter or break off part of the airplane by accident. When this happens, the planes don't fly as well as they are designed to. Life is delicate, like the balsa plane. When we break in the right areas we will fly higher and smoother than when we break in the wrong places. . . .

When we are broken in the wrong places, we become self-centered. Our broken emotions keep us from loving effectively. We shun future settings where further hurt could take place, like significant relationships, churches, and goal-setting. Or we react defensively to the hurt by overachieving and living a life of abandon. . . . When we are broken in the wrong places, we do not see the fruit of the Spirit.

Look around you. The older you get, the more you see people who have lost the twinkle in their eyes. They have endured tough circumstances, but not successfully. . . . Being broken in the heart, in the soul, where God can do something with your will and character, is a matter of converting, sanctifying the actual pain, and making it a part of the healing salve. You cannot do it on your own. God must. But you must be willing.

Aging, Fear, Self-centeredness, Testing, Trials
Ps. 51:17; Rom. 5:2–5; James 1:2–4

Date used _____ Place _____

Change   18

Jan Riggenbach writes a newspaper column on gardening. In an article she wrote about how to plant bedding plants, we learn something about Christian growth.

"Giving new bedding plants some rough treatment at planting time," she says, "may be the best thing you can do to help them survive in the garden. When I was new to gardening, I tried to set tomatoes, petunias, and other bedding plants in the garden without disturbing their roots at all. Nowadays, I'm much more ruthless. . . ."

Riggenbach says she squeezes the bottoms of the flexible plastic pots to get the plants out of their container and then she inspects the soil ball.

"If the plant has been growing in its pot so long that the roots are circling the bottom," says Riggenbach, "I jab my finger into the bottom of the soil and pull down to untangle the roots. . . . If the whole pot is filled with circling roots, I have to be merciless. I don't worry if I break some of the roots; that's better than allowing the roots to continue to circle when the plants are growing in the garden. Most bedding plants shrug off this rough treatment."

Christians often resemble rootbound plants. We grow complacent and comfortable where we are. Our roots circle around and around in the same small area, no longer reaching out for life and nourishment and growth. The healthiest thing God can do for us is shake up our roots and put us in new soil.

Comfort, Complacency, Discipline, Fruitfulness, Growth
John 15:1–8

Date used _____ Place _____

In the *South Shore News,* Kathleen Kroll Driscoll was writing about dating and how a woman can figure out what kind of person she's going out with.

She says:

> A theater is an interesting place to analyze someone new in your life. Does he have a phobia about sitting on the aisle? When everyone else is sniffling and crying, is he busy unwrapping licorice and covering up emotions? Does he hog the communal armrest? Does he put his feet on the seat in front? Is he reluctant to ask people to move over one seat so the two of you can sit together? Everything you want to know about your potential mate can be discerned during a movie.

Who we really are cannot be hidden. And the little things often reveal the most.

Discernment, Fruits, Testing
Matt. 12:33–37; 1 Tim. 3:10

Date used _____ Place _____

A computer virus on the loose is a computer user's worst nightmare. A virus can destroy everything in a computer's memory. According to S&S Software International and writer James Coates, here is how a computer virus works.

> A computer virus is software, or a piece of programming code, whose purpose is to replicate. . . . Many viruses enter the computer via a floppy disk or are downloaded from another source. . . . Once the computer is infected, the virus checks each time a program is opened to see if the program is clean. If it is, the virus copies itself onto the program. Because viruses need time to spread undetected, most will not affect the proper functioning of the computer right away.

But eventually their destructive power is felt as files are erased or corrupted.

Just as a computer virus spreads through the files of a computer, so sin can spread in the church.

Holiness, Intervention, Spiritual sickness
1 Cor. 5; Gal. 6:1

Date used _____ Place _____

28

Commitment

In his newspaper column called "Market Report," Bill Barn-hart once explained the difference between investors and traders in the stock market.

"A trader in a stock," writes Barnhart, "is making decisions minute-by-minute in the hope of shaving off profits measured in fractions of a dollar. . . . An investor, on the other hand, typically buys or sells a stock based on views about the company and the economy at large."

In other words, traders are wheelers and dealers. They pursue short-term profits. Traders may have no confidence whatsoever in the companies in which they buy stock but they buy, smelling an immediate payoff.

By contrast, investors are in it for the long haul. They "chain themselves to the mast." Investors commit their money to a stock, believing that over a period of years and even decades the stock will pay strong dividends and steadily grow in value. Investors aren't flustered by the typical ups and downs of the market because they believe in the quality of the company, its leaders, and its product.

In the kingdom of God there are also investors and traders. They come to Christ with very different goals. Traders in the kingdom want God to improve their lot in this world. If following Christ means pain or hardship, they sell out.

But investors in the kingdom stay true to Christ no matter what happens in this world, knowing that eternal dividends await them.

Eternal, Feelings, Rewards, Suffering, Temporal
Mark 4:1–20

Date used _____ Place _____

Communion

At the Vietnam Veterans Memorial, that long wall of black marble engraved with the names of those killed in the war, people come to remember their friends and loved ones. Writer Don Moser says that often they leave tokens of their remembrance: flags, sealed letters, pieces of clothing, photos. Volunteers collect these tokens daily and store them at the Vietnam Veterans Memorial Collection.

A book called *Offerings at the Wall* pictures many of these mementos. One man left dog tags, a headband, and a letter that reads, "To all of you here from Echo Company, 1st Marine Regiment, 1st Marine Division . . . I leave you my headband which contains my sweat from the war, my dog tag, and a picture of me and Mike. Another time, another place. I'll never forget you."

A woman left a braid of hair and a picture of a house with an American flag hanging at the porch. Her note read, "Wayne, I think of you every day and miss you so much. I love you."

Written on one flag was this message: "May all of you who died, all of you still missing, and all of you who returned home never be forgotten—Connie."

It's important that we remember. Jesus told us what tokens he wants us to use to remember his death: the bread and the cup. Each has deep meaning for those who love our risen Lord.

Lord's Supper, Memorial, Remembrance
1 Cor. 11:23–26

Date used _____ Place _____

In October of 1993, in the town of Worcester, Massachusetts, police found an old woman dead on her kitchen floor. This was no ordinary discovery—she had been dead four years. Police speculated she died at age seventy-three of natural causes. That's when her bank transactions ended.

How can someone be so cut off from relationships that no one even notices when he or she dies?

To some extent, it was a mistake. According to the Associated Press, four years earlier, neighbors had called authorities when they sensed something might be wrong. When the police contacted the woman's brother, he said she had gone into a nursing home. Police told the postal service to stop delivering mail. One neighbor paid her grandson to cut the grass because the place was looking run-down. Another neighbor had the utility company come and shut off the water when a pipe froze, broke, and sent water spilling out the door.

To a great extent, though, it was not a mistake.

One friend from the past said, "She didn't want anyone bothering her at all. I guess she got her wish, but it's awfully sad."

Her brother said the family hadn't been close since their mother died in 1979. He added, "Someone should have noticed something before now."

The woman had lived in her house in this middle-class neighborhood for forty years, but none of her neighbors knew her well. "My heart bleeds for her," said the woman who lives across the street. "But you can't blame a soul. If she saw you out there, she never said hello to you."

As this neighborhood shows, a spirit of community only results when all of us reach out to one another. Relationships take effort.

Communication, Family, Friendship
Heb. 10:25; 1 John 1:7

Date used _____ Place _____

In March of 1994 a German tourist checked into a hotel near Miami International Airport. That night in his room he noticed a foul odor. But travelers must put up with discomforts, so he slept in the bed that night without a complaint to the front desk.

The next morning when he awoke, the odor was only worse. So as he checked out of the hotel, he reported the problem. On Friday, March 11, a maid cleaning the room discovered the source of the odor. Under the bed she found a corpse.

Life is filled with problems, and often it seems the best thing to do is just ignore them. But if we realized how serious and close some problems really are, we would take action.

Apathy, Change, Problems, Repentance
Prov. 1:32; Jer. 6:13–14; 2 Cor. 6:1–2

Date used _____ Place _____

In his book *Identity: Youth and Crisis*, Erik Erikson tells a story he heard from a physician about an old man with a peculiar problem. The old man vomited every morning but had never felt any inclination to consult a doctor. Finally the man's family convinced him to get a checkup.

The doctor asked, "How are you?"

"I'm fine," the man responded. "Couldn't be better."

The doctor examined him and found he was in good shape for his age.

Finally the physician grew impatient and asked, "I hear that you vomit every morning."

The old man looked surprised and said, "Sure. Doesn't everybody?"

Like that old man, we may not realize that the problems we bear daily are abnormal. We've lived with the problems for so long we can't imagine how life could be better.

Abundant life, Problems, Sin
John 10:10

Date used _____ Place _____

Workers for the Chicago Transit Authority have minted some interesting terms to describe life on the trains and tracks of the city, says writer Anne Keegan.

The elevated train often runs on a platform built above the city streets. In many places, these platforms are narrow, with just enough width for two trains to pass. If a workman was fixing the tracks when two trains came from different directions, he would have no room to avoid the oncoming trains.

And so, now and then alongside the tracks there is a small platform with a railing, three feet square, projecting out over the street. These small platforms provide a place for those working on the tracks to escape an oncoming train.

Workers for the Chicago Transit Authority call these platforms "fool catchers."

On occasion we all play the fool. We lose our temper or bend the truth or neglect our responsibilities or perhaps even do something criminal. We make decisions that in hindsight we realize were just plain stupid. As the trains of trouble come bearing down on us, we need to remember that God has provided a way of escape. The fool catcher is confession.

Foolishness, Mistakes, Sin
Ps. 51; Prov. 28:13; Luke 18:9–14; 1 John 1:8–10

Date used _____ Place _____

Conversion

Not many conversion stories make it to the pages of the *Wall Street Journal,* but Dr. Marvin Overton's did. A June 6, 1994, article by Robert Johnson shows how true it is that when a person accepts Christ, all things become new.

Dr. Marvin Overton is one of the finest brain surgeons in the nation, a past-president of the Texas Association of Neurosurgeons. In 1992 he began attending a small church in Burnet, Texas, and had a spiritual awakening. About the same time, he began suffering severe, lingering pain in his abdomen. X rays eventually revealed cancer. Several days after the diagnosis, however, tests showed nothing, and Overton has felt fine ever since. Overton was completely healed. The healing crystallized his born-again experience.

Before his conversion he was a skeptic and a rationalist who believed in the power of science. Now, says the *Journal,* Overton has "more answers than questions, a granite certitude about the mind, the brain, and the soul."

Before his conversion he was, by his own description, cold-hearted. "I was a good surgeon," said Overton, "but I was coarse. I couldn't shed a tear. My attitude [toward patients] was 'tough.'"

Now he writes notes to friends, notes containing encouraging quotes from Scripture, and he cares enough about patients to ask those scheduled for surgery, "If something goes wrong, are you comfortable that you know God and that you'll go to heaven?"

Before Overton's conversion his god was wine. Not that he was an alcoholic; rather, he owned one of the finest wine collections in the country, over ten thousand bottles of every important vintage made between the late 1700s and 1930. His collection was valued at more than a million dollars. Dr. Overton threw wine-tasting banquets for which French chefs, and hand-carried bottles, were flown in by a Concorde jet. "Wine had become my idol," said Overton. "I worshipped the god Bacchus. . . . I was an excellent heathen."

After Overton's conversion he sold his wine collection, giving much of the proceeds to charity.

Before his conversion Overton was a Fort Worth socialite. Now he is one of the leaders in his small-town, blue-collar church in Burnet, Texas. He even goes door-to-door to tell others about Christ.

What has impressed others most is not his healing but his life. "The question of whether he got an incorrect diagnosis, or whatever, really doesn't matter," said Michael McWhorter, chairman of the American Association of Neurological Surgeons science board. "Who are we to say a miracle didn't happen? Something changed his life."

When a person becomes a fully devoted follower of Jesus Christ, all things become new.

Healing, Witness
John 3:3; 2 Cor. 5:17

Date used _____ Place _____

Campus Life magazine told the conversion story of singer Kathy Troccoli. She grew up with an overprotective mother, and as Kathy got older, she rebelled, abusing alcohol and suffering eating disorders.

Says Kathy, "Maybe you've heard the phrase, 'We are as sick as our secrets.' I was real sick."

While Kathy started out rebelling against an overprotective mom, she wound up rebelling against herself—and at the expense of her own health and self-esteem. Into this swirl of rebellion and alcohol and unhappiness, Jesus came—in the form of a nerd.

At the time, Kathy was partying with her friends and singing in clubs by night.

By day, she was working her summer job at a community pool, and Cindy was her prissy co-worker who read the Bible every day during lunch.

"She was the epitome of a girl that I would not hang out with," says Kathy. "I hung out with harder girls. Tougher. Cindy was kind of frilly. Pink—she was like a pink girl. And when she started telling me about Jesus, I made fun of her. And yet, somewhere deep down inside, I admired her. I was intrigued by her boldness. I liked it that she didn't seem to care what people thought about her. I even suspected she was right, and that I was on the wrong path."

Kathy knew the truth of Christianity hung by a thin thread called faith. She knew there were unanswerable questions, and day after day she fired those questions at frilly Cindy, the Jesus nerd. Finally, one answer, one statement from the pink girl got through. "She said, 'You know, Kath, Jesus is Lord whether you accept him or not.' I went home thinking about that," says Kathy. "I did have this growing sense that if Jesus was real, I had to check him out."

Cindy obliged, giving Kathy a small New Testament. "My other friends thought I was weird," says Kathy, "because I was taking this Bible home, but I did, unapologetically. I read the

Gospel of John, plowing right on through, despite a few unanswered questions. When I got to the end, I knew I had to make
a decision. If Jesus was who he said he was, I would have to
respond. Everything would have to change."
  On August 5th [1988], it did.
  Everything changed.
  Or rather, the changes began.

Addictions, Boldness, Evangelism
2 Cor. 5:17; 1 Thess. 2:3–8

Date used _____ Place _____

From *Campus Life* Magazine, copyright © 1994, published by Christianity Today, Inc.,
Carol Stream, Ill. Used by permission.

In his book *Enjoying God*, Lloyd Ogilvie writes about the conversion of a fellow student named Allistair.

One summer while finishing his doctoral program, [Allistair] had a carrel next to mine in the library. Often we lunched together and shared thoughtful discussions about faith. Allistair had little experience with the church and had not made a profession of faith in Christ. . . .

Several times our discussions brought Allistair to the edge of the decision to become a Christian. Then he would back off. One day our lunch discussion focused on grace. Near the end of our conversation, I took out my pen and placed it on the table.

"Allistair," I said, "you need to make a decision. When you decide to accept the gift of grace and commit your life to Christ, pick up the pen. . . ."

Allistair sat for more than an hour staring at the pen.

During this time a mutual Scots friend who enjoys God came over to our table. He noticed that we had been silently sitting for a long time.

"What are you lads doing?" he asked with a chuckle.

Allistair looked up and replied intently, "I'm trying to decide whether to become a Christian."

Sensing the intensity of the moment, our friend said, "Why not do it now and get on with your life?" and walked away.

Allistair returned to his silent meditation. I waited and prayed.

Suddenly, as if propelled by an inner compunction, Allistair thrust out his hand and grasped the pen.

"Now is none too soon!" he exclaimed with joy.

God has provided a way for us to have eternal life through Jesus Christ, but we must accept it.

Evangelism, Procrastination, Receiving Christ
John 1:12; 2 Cor. 6:1–2

Date used _____ Place _____

Used by permission of the publisher.

Economist Robert Eggert began a monthly newsletter called *Blue Chip Economic Indicators* in 1976, and it is now read by the American president, the chairman of the Federal Reserve, and CEOs of the biggest companies in America. The newsletter attempts to predict the future.

Blue Chip Economic Indicators gives forecasts on economic matters like gross domestic product growth and unemployment rates. How does Robert Eggert and the *Blue Chip* predict the future with an accuracy that motivates subscribers to pay a subscription rate of $498 a year?

Eggert's secret is a simple idea he got in 1969: He gives a consensus forecast. Writer Mark Memmott describes the process:

> On the 15th of each month, he sends a memo to the 75 economists on his list. They include forecasters at such household names as Ford, Chrysler, General Motors, Sears and J. P. Morgan, academics from UCLA and Georgia State, and consultants. He alerts them to special questions he'll be asking. Then, on the first working day of each month, his questionnaires are faxed to all 75.
>
> By the fifth working day of the month, Eggert has crunched the responses, written his analysis and sent the copy to the publisher.

Eggert first experimented with his idea of making a consensus forecast in the early seventies when he was chief economist for RCA. "When I started to average out [other economists'] forecasts, it became apparent the consensus usually had an almost uncanny ability to predict what was coming."

Solomon put it this way: "A wise man listens to advice" (Prov. 12:15).

Advice, Consensus, Decisions, Leadership, Plans, Wisdom
Prov. 12:15; 15:22

Date used _____ Place _____

Anything that is extremely valuable will be counterfeited.

Fake gems have been around for thousands of years, but as the technology for making them has advanced, fakes are now harder to detect with the naked eye.

Gem buyers today must be aware of three types of gems that are made to look more valuable than they are.

1. *Synthetic gems,* says writer Vivian Marino, are "lab-grown stones that closely duplicate a natural gem's physical and chemical properties."
2. *Simulated gems* are also manmade. The color of a simulated stone may be similar to that of a natural gem, but it is very different physically and chemically. "Cubic zirconia is a well-known diamond simulation."
3. *Enhanced gems* are natural gems altered in some way to improve their look. "Color can be enhanced through heat, radiation, oils, and chemicals." Other methods used to imitate or enhance the value of stones are "dyeing, waxing, or smoking poor quality stones to make them look richer."

Experts advise buyers to verify a stone's value with gem-testing labs, such as the Gemological Institute of America, before any sales are final. When paying big money for jewels, you want to be very careful about getting the genuine article.

It is the same with truth. We must ensure we are not falling for heresy.

Appearance, Authenticity, Character, Deception, False prophets,
Gospel, Heresy, Integrity, Orthodoxy, Truth
Matt. 7:15–23; 2 Cor. 11:13–15; Gal. 1:6–9; 1 Tim. 3:10

Date used _____ Place _____

Rosa Parks, mother of the civil rights movement, was arrested in 1955 for refusing to give her bus seat to a white man. Boycotts and protests followed, and eventually the Supreme Court ruled racial segregation unconstitutional. In *Quiet Strength* she writes:

> I have learned over the years that knowing what must be done does away with fear. When I sat down on the bus that day, I had no idea history was being made—I was only thinking of getting home. But I had made up my mind. After so many years of being a victim of the mistreatment my people suffered, not giving up my seat—and whatever I had to face afterwards—was not important. I did not feel any fear sitting there. I felt the Lord would give me the strength to endure whatever I had to face. It was time for someone to stand up—or in my case, sit down. So I refused to move.

Settle in your mind what is right, and you will find courage in your heart.

Determination, Fear, Leadership, Righteousness
Prov. 28:1; Matt. 5:6

Date used _____ Place _____

Twenty-seven people are banking on the idea that modern science will someday find or engineer a fountain of youth. Those twenty-seven people, all deceased, are "patients" of the Alcor Life Extension Institute in Scottsdale, Arizona, where their bodies—or merely their heads!—have been frozen in liquid nitrogen at minus 320 degrees Fahrenheit awaiting the day when medical science discovers a way to make death and aging a thing of the past.

Ten of the patients paid $120,000 to have their entire body frozen. Seventeen of the patients paid $50,000 to have only their head frozen, hoping that molecular technology will one day be able to grow a whole new body from their head or its cells.

It sounds like science fiction, but it's called cryonics.

As you can imagine, cryonics has its share of critics and skeptics. And of course, Stephen Bridge, president of Alcor, cautions, "We have to tell [people] that we don't even really know if it will work yet."

Nevertheless Thomas Donaldson, a fifty-year-old member of Alcor who hasn't yet taken advantage of its services, brushed aside the naysayers and explained to a reporter why he's willing to give cryonics a try: "For some strange reason, I like being alive. . . . I don't want to die. Okay, guys?"

For those, like Donaldson, who like being alive, God has good news. Jesus Christ has risen from the dead with an eternal, resurrection body. He has conquered death. All those who believe in Jesus will someday also be raised from the dead with an eternal resurrection body. Jesus is the only sure hope of eternal life.

Easter, Hope, Resurrection, Science
John 11:25; 1 Cor. 15

Date used _____ Place _____

In his book *Broken in the Right Place*, Alan Nelson quotes Paul Cedar:

In the early 1970s, God called us clearly to leave a very blessed pastoral ministry we were carrying on in Southern California to begin a nonprofit ministry which had a particular focus on reaching out and ministering to pastors and local churches. The new ministry was going exceedingly well. However, the "cash flow" was not. . . .

In addition, the enemy brought other attacks upon us which brought embarrassment, discouragement, disillusionment—and even humiliation. . . .

On a given evening, while I was driving alone in my car en route to a ministry engagement, I cried out to God in pain and frustration. . . . I rehearsed for Him all of the sacrifices that we had made for Him in obedience to Him. I reminded Him of the embarrassment and humiliation which we had experienced. Finally, in utter despair I cried out, "Lord, why don't you just take my life!" Immediately, I sensed He was speaking to me in a loving, tender way like a faithful father wanting what was best for His son. I sensed Him saying to me, "Son, I already have taken your life."

Immediately, I was broken before God. I pulled over to the side of the road and sobbed uncontrollably in praise and adoration before God.

Indeed I had given my total life to Him a number of years before. I was His to do whatever He chose to do with. It was at that time on that particular evening that I committed myself anew to die to self and to be alive to God. I so committed my life to Christ that if He chose for me to be a failure, I would attempt to even do that to His glory!

> Brokenness, Commitment, Failure, Sacrifice
> Rom. 6:12–23; Gal. 2:20

Date used _____ Place _____

Used by permission of the publisher.

Nichelle Nichols played Uhura in the original *Star Trek* TV program and six *Star Trek* movies. She was one of the first Black women regularly featured on a weekly TV show. As such, she had obstacles to overcome. According to Steve Jones in *USA Today*, a few studio executives were hostile toward her character, which was often diminished by script rewrites, and the studio even withheld tons of her fan mail. After one year on the program, she was fed up. Nichols, who was also an extremely talented professional singer and dancer, told Gene Roddenberry she was going to quit and pursue her performing career.

Before she did, however, she went to a fundraiser for the NAACP. There she happened to meet Dr. Martin Luther King, who urged her not to leave the show. She was a role model for many.

Says Nichols, "When you have a man like Dr. Martin Luther King say you can't leave a show, it's daunting. It humbled my heart, and I couldn't leave. God had charged me with something more important than my own career."

The rest, as they say, is history. Not only did she become a fixture on *Star Trek*, she actually influenced NASA, challenging them to hire Blacks and women for their astronaut corps. She led a 1977 NASA recruitment drive that saw 1,600 women and 1,000 minorities apply within four months.

By giving up her plans to sing and dance, Nichols found the defining role of her career—Uhura—in one of the most popular TV shows ever and influenced a nation.

Like Nichelle Nichols, as we die to ourselves and our own plans so that we can pursue something far more important—the cause of Christ—we find our God-given destiny.

Ministry, Perseverance, Sacrifice, Selfishness, Service
John 12:24–26; 1 Cor. 15:58; Gal. 2:20; 6:9–10

Date used _____ Place _____

In his sermon "Overcoming Discouragement," John Yates says:

> Dr. Karl Menninger, the famous psychiatrist, once gave a lecture on mental health and was answering questions from the audience. Someone said, "What would you advise a person to do if that person felt a nervous breakdown coming on?"
>
> Most people thought he would say, "Go see a psychiatrist immediately," but he didn't. To their astonishment, Dr. Menninger replied, "Lock up your house, go across the railroad tracks, find somebody in need, and help that person."

To overcome discouragement, "Don't focus on yourself," concluded Yates. "Get involved in the lives of other people."

Emotions, Giving, Love, Mental health, Ministry
Acts 20:35

Date used _____ Place _____

Alvin Straight, age seventy-three, lived in Laurens, Iowa. His brother, age eighty, lived several hundred miles away in Blue River, Wisconsin. According to the Associated Press, Alvin's brother had suffered a stroke, and Alvin wanted to see him, but he had a transportation problem. He didn't have a driver's license because his eyesight was bad and he apparently had an aversion to taking a plane, train, or bus.

But Alvin didn't let that stop him. In 1994 he climbed aboard his 1966 John Deere tractor lawn mower and drove it all the way to Blue River, Wisconsin.

Devotion finds a way.

Brotherly love, Commitment, Persistence, Sacrifice
Rom. 12:10; 2 Tim. 1:16–18

Date used _____ Place _____

According to Reuters news agency, Daniel Lehner and his wife, Remy, were married December 12, 1993. Evidently they believe in doing up anniversaries in a big, big way. Before they even celebrated their first anniversary, they made plans for how they would celebrate their second. They made plans to go to one of their favorite plays—*The Phantom of the Opera,* by Andrew Lloyd Webber—which they had already seen many times.

But just going to the play was not enough to express their love. They wanted to make a grand gesture. So, more than a year in advance, they bought tickets for every seat in the house of New York's Majestic Theater for December 12, 1995. That's 1,609 seats.

With that date still more than a year away, how do you think they celebrated their first anniversary? That's right. They went to see *The Phantom of the Opera.*

Daniel and Remy evidently love each other—and this play—deeply. As they have demonstrated, one of the marks of passionate love is extravagance.

When Jesus walked the earth, there were people who expressed their love to him with extravagance, and Jesus calls us today to love him with extravagant love.

Extravagance, Love for God, Marriage, Worship
2 Sam. 6:14–16; Matt. 16:24–26; Mark 12:30; John 12:1–3; Rom. 12:1

Date used _____ Place _____

Devotional Life

In the 1994 Winter Olympics, held in Norway, twenty-three-year-old Tommy Moe of the United States won the gold on the men's downhill. It was "a beautifully controlled run," said William Oscar Johnson in *Sports Illustrated,* "on which he held tucks and thrust his hands forward in perfect form at places where others had stood up and flailed their arms."

After his victory, Tommy Moe explained his thought processes. "I kept it simple," he said, "focused on skiing, not on winning, not on where I'd place. I remembered to breathe—sometimes I don't."

The winner of the gold medal in the Olympics had to remember the most basic of basics: breathing! He kept it simple.

Likewise as we seek to have a strong walk with God, it doesn't take a rocket scientist to know where we win or lose. Spiritual strength depends on the basics. We need to make sure we're breathing the things of the Spirit.

Basics, Church, Holy Spirit, Prayer, Spiritual disciplines
Gal. 5:16–26; 1 Thess. 5:16–22; 1 Peter 2:2; Jude 20

Date used _____ Place _____

George O. Wood writes that on October 31, 1983, Korean Airlines flight 007 departed from Anchorage, Alaska, for a direct flight to Seoul, Korea. Unknown to the crew, however, the computer engaging the flight navigation system contained a one-and-a-half-degree routing error. At the point of departure, the mistake was unnoticeable. One hundred miles out, the deviation was still so small as to be undetectable. But as the giant 747 continued through the Aleutians and out over the Pacific, the plane strayed increasingly from its proper course. Eventually it was flying over Soviet air space.

Soviet radar picked up the error, and fighter jets scrambled into the air to intercept. Over mainland Russia the jets shot flight 007 out of the sky, and all aboard lost their lives.

Choose your direction well. Although poor choices may hurt you in only minor ways for a while, the longer you go, the more harm they bring.

Beginnings, Commitment, Compromise,
Doctrine, Goals, God's will, Priorities
Prov. 4:25–26; Luke 9:57–62; Rom. 12:2; Phil. 3:7–11; 1 Peter 1:13

Date used _____ Place _____

In 1995 Jane Brody reported in the *New York Times* that Boston researchers had demonstrated for the first time that the eye has two functions.

"Just as the human ear controls both hearing and balance," she writes, "the eye . . . not only permits conscious vision but also independently registers light impulses that regulate the body's internal daily clock. Even people who are totally blind and have no perception of light can have normal hormonal responses to bright light." This second function of the eye, which regulates the body's twenty-four-hour clock, keeps in order our biological rhythms, such as sleep.

"Light passes through the retina and travels through a special tract in the optic nerves to a region of the brain called the suprachiasmatic nucleus, the brain's pacemaker. The light impulses then go on to the pineal gland, stopping to release a hormone called melatonin. Melatonin, the so-called hormone of darkness, normally reaches a peak in the blood at night when the lights are out. But when bright light is shown in the eyes, melatonin production shuts down."

According to Jesus, the eye—that is, the eye of the soul—has a third function: "Your eye is the lamp of your body. When your eyes are good, your whole body also is full of light. But when they are bad, your body also is full of darkness. See to it, then, that the light within you is not darkness" (Luke 11:34–35).

The eye of the soul has both moral and spiritual sensibilities, allowing in spiritual darkness or light. As the human body responds to light and darkness, so the human spirit responds to the spiritual light and darkness in our world.

Discernment, Entertainment, Interests, Lust, Morality, Worldliness
Prov. 17:24; Luke 11:34–35; 1 Cor. 2:15–16

Date used _____ Place _____

In the 1994 Winter Olympics held in Norway, twenty-three-year-old skier Tommy Moe of the United States captured the gold on the men's downhill. It marked a big comeback for Tommy.

He had shown great potential for years but according to *Sports Illustrated*, had a penchant for smoking pot and drinking. In 1986 as a fifteen year old, he was invited to be a part of the U.S. ski team, but when the coaches learned that he had sneaked out of camp to smoke pot, they kicked him off the team.

Tommy's father, an Alaskan construction worker, decided his son needed some discipline and he ordered him to come to Alaska. There he put Tommy to work.

Tommy was on the job at 4 A.M. and he labored under the Alaskan sun for twelve to sixteen hours a day during the long days of Arctic summer. "I worked his rear end off," says Tom Sr. "And then I asked him if he'd rather be doing this or if he'd rather be skiing with the team in Argentina. That straightened him out."

Tommy recalls, "It was mental torture, bad news. It humbled me up pretty fast."

He got serious about ski racing pretty quickly.

Fathers know that children sometimes need discipline and that discipline is hard. But it yields big results.

God the Father, Humility, Sloth
Prov. 6:6–11; Heb. 12:5–13

Date used _____ Place _____

Shaping a child's character is a bit like stone carving.

Smithsonian magazine once did a feature on a master stone carver from England named Simon Verity. Verity learned stone carving by restoring thirteenth-century cathedrals in Great Britain. The four basic tools of his trade are a hammer, a punch, a chisel, and a rasp.

The authors who interviewed Verity and watched him work noticed something interesting.

"Verity listens closely to hear the song of the stone under his careful blows," they write. "A solid strike and all is well. A higher pitched ping and it could mean trouble; a chunk of rock could break off. He constantly adjusts the angle of the chisel and the force of the mallet to the pitch, pausing frequently to run his hand over the freshly carved surface."

In the same way, when parents discipline a child, they must listen with great sensitivity to how the child responds.

Child rearing, Fathers
Eph. 6:4; Col. 3:21

Date used _____ Place _____

The cowbird is unique in North America. While some other birds will occasionally lay their eggs in other birds' nests, the cowbird does so exclusively. In Illinois, for example, the little brown cowbird with its mink-colored head is a common sight, but bird experts say you will not find one cowbird nest in the entire state.

And that's becoming a problem, says writer Peter Kendall. The cowbirds are

> prodigious egg-layers: Each female commonly deposits 20 to 40 eggs in dozens of other nests each spring. Cowbird eggs usually hatch more quickly than the other bird's eggs, and the chicks grow more quickly. Because birds tend to feed the largest and loudest of their young first—because they usually would be the healthiest and have the best chance of survival—the host bird spends inordinate time and energy tending to the cowbird.

As a result the cowbird is pushing some other songbirds to extinction.

Like the cowbird, distractions in our lives have a way of intruding themselves and taking over. Distractions can cause the extinction of godly activities.

Church, Devotional life, Entertainment, Habits, Priorities
Luke 14:15–24; Heb. 10:24–25; 12:1–2

Date used _____ Place _____

The late jazz trumpeter Dizzy Gillespie is remembered not only for his talent but also for how his cheeks puffed out like a frog's as he blew his horn.

Writer Jim Doherty says that one day Gillespie was talking with Chicago Symphony trumpeter Adolph (Bud) Herseth. Herseth, a White man, is known for turning beet red when he plays. Gillespie, who was Black, kidded with Herseth, "Bud, how come your cheeks don't puff out when you play?"

Herseth replied, "Diz, how come your face doesn't get red when you play?"

Two great trumpeters. Two different styles. God has made us all unique, and creation shouts the message that God enjoys that diversity.

Acceptance, Creation, Harmony, Prejudice, Uniqueness
Gen. 1–2; Rom. 12:16; 1 Cor. 12

Date used _____ Place _____

Baseball slugger Mickey Mantle is a tragic picture of how alcohol abuse can destroy what we value most. After treatment at the Betty Ford center, Mantle went public with his story of forty-two years of alcohol abuse. For a man blessed with incredible strength, ability, and good things in life, it is a story of loss.

Alcohol destroyed Mantle's mind. "I could be talking to you and just completely forget my train of thought . . . ," says Mantle. "I'd forget what day it was, what month it was, what city I was in."

Alcohol destroyed Mantle's peace of mind. "I had these weird hangovers—bad anxiety attacks . . . ," he writes. "There were times when I locked myself in my bedroom to feel safe."

Alcohol destroyed Mantle's body. "The doctor . . . said, 'Before long you're just going to have one big scab for a liver,'" recalls Mantle. "'Eventually you'll need a new liver. . . . The next drink you take might be your last.'"

Alcohol diminished Mantle as a baseball player. "The drinking shortened my career . . . ," says Mantle. "Casey [Stengel] had said when I came up, 'This guy's going to be better than Joe DiMaggio and Babe Ruth.' It didn't happen. God gave me a great body to play with, and I didn't take care of it."

Alcohol robbed Mantle of a deep relationship with his four sons. "One of the things I really screwed up, besides baseball," he writes, "was being a father. I wasn't a good family man. I was always out, running around with the guys."

When God warns us against drunkenness, he isn't a spoil sport; he's a lifesaver.

Addictions, Chemical dependency, Commands, Regret
Eph. 5:18

Date used _____ Place _____

Harvey Penick was the golf coach at the University of Texas from 1931 to 1963 and the golf mentor for some of the greats: Ben Crenshaw, Tom Kite, Kathy Whitworth, Betsy Rawls, and Mickey Wright. They returned to Penick even after years on the pro golfers' circuit to seek his help with their putting, chipping, and driving.

Like any good coach, Penick was a careful observer who learned how to golf from watching others. In fact, for decades Penick scribbled his random observations about golf into a notebook. One day he mentioned these golf diaries to a writer named Bud Shrake. Shrake saw the publishing potential in Penick's notebooks and collaborated with him on a book published in 1992 under the title *Harvey Penick's Little Red Book: Lessons and Teachings from a Lifetime in Golf*. The *Little Red Book* sold more than a million copies, becoming the best-selling sports book in history. Penick was eighty-seven years old.

Most older people haven't written a *Little Red Book,* but like Penick observing golfers, they've observed life and learned important things the hard way. A wise person takes seriously the wisdom of older people.

Counsel, Leaders, Learning, Teachability, Wisdom
1 Peter 5:5

Date used _____ Place _____

In June of 1993 the police in South Windsor, Connecticut, pulled over motorists in larger numbers than usual, but not because scofflaws had overrun the city.

One person stopped by a patrolman was Lori Carlson, according to the Reuters news service. As the policeman approached her car, she wondered what she had done wrong. To her amazement the officer handed her a ticket that said, "Your driving was GREAT!—and we appreciate it."

On Wednesday, June 9, the authorities in this Hartford suburb had begun a new program to give safe drivers a two-dollar reward for obeying the speed limit, wearing safety belts, having children in protective seats, and using turn signals.

"You are always nervous when you see the police lights come on," said Carl Lomax, another resident of South Windsor pulled over for good driving. "It takes a second or two to adjust to the officer saying, 'Hey, thanks a lot for obeying the law.' It's about the last thing you would expect."

The police of South Windsor had a good idea. The first thing others should expect from us is encouragement. Our friends, family, and fellow workers will respond best if we not only correct them when they do wrong but thank them for doing right.

Parenting, Relationships, Thanks
1 Thess. 5:11

Date used _____ Place _____

According to the Reuters news agency, in the late 1980s a Hong Kong man was walking near a military firing range when he found a 66-mm anti-tank rocket. He was a gun enthusiast, so he brought it home. He polished the live rocket, which contained twelve ounces of high explosive, and placed it on top of his television.

One day during a probe of attempted robbery charges, the police searched the twenty-two-year-old man's apartment and found and confiscated the rocket. Had the rocket ever fired, it would have demolished the apartment.

Why would someone willfully bring such a deadly force into his living room? Few people have explosives *on top* of their televisions, but many have deadly spiritual weapons *in* their televisions. They bring spiritual danger to themselves and their family when they turn on the tube, because they watch programs that can destroy their values.

Television, Thoughts, Values, Violence
Prov. 4:23; Rom. 12:1–2; Phil. 4:8; 1 John 2:15–17

Date used _____ Place _____

Evangelism

In the spring of 1992 fourth-grade students in Portland, Maine, carried out a novel experiment. Their teacher, Pamela Trieu, was teaching the kids about the ocean, specifically about the Gulf Stream that flows along the East Coast and then turns toward Europe. According to Reuters, she had the kids put messages with their addresses in empty wine bottles, and then a fisherman took the twenty-one bottles away from shore and threw them into the ocean. They hoped that some of the bottles might drift to England.

Three months later, two bottles washed up in Canada. The class heard nothing else and assumed that the rest of the bottles were lost at sea. Two years passed. Then one of the students, Geoff Hight, received a surprise letter from a girl in Pornichet, France. She found one of their bottles while walking with her father on the beach.

Our efforts at evangelism are often like tossing a bottle with a message into the ocean. We share the gospel with others however we can—giving them a piece of literature, a personal testimony, a prayer with someone in need. We see no response and think our message is forgotten, "lost at sea." But years later we learn that the Spirit of God—like the mighty Gulf Stream—has carried our message to its destination.

Gospel, Patience
Isa. 55:10–11; Rom. 1:16

Date used _____ Place _____

In *Leadership*, Graham R. Hodges writes:

When I was a boy milking several cows each morning and night, I dreaded the cocklebur season. In late summer, this prolific weed turned brown, and its seed pods, each armed with dozens of sharp spines, caught in the cows' tails until the animals' fly switchers were transformed into mean whips. One hard switch of such a tail in the milker's face made him lose considerable religion.

So I learned to hate the cocklebur.

Later, comfortably removed from the dairy industry, I learned a remarkable fact about the cocklebur: its sticky seed pod contains several seeds, not just one. And these seeds germinate in different years. Thus, if seed *A* fails to sprout next year because of a drought, seed *B* will be there waiting for the year after next, and seed *C* the year after that, waiting until the right conditions for germination arrive.

Hodges says the genius of the cocklebur pod is much like that of the spiritual seeds we plant in the lives of others. People don't always respond to God's Word immediately. But the seed is planted, and when the time is ripe, it will bring a harvest.

Patience, Reaping, Seeds, Sowing
Isa. 55:10–11; John 4:35–38; Gal. 6:9–10

Date used _____ Place _____

According to the Associated Press, on June 4, 1961, the K–19, a Soviet nuclear submarine, was conducting a training exercise in the North Atlantic when a pipe carrying coolant to the nuclear reactor burst. In the reactor room the temperature quickly soared to 140 degrees, and the radiation level mounted. The reactor had to be cooled or it would burst, poisoning the sea with radiation.

The captain of the sub, Nikolai Zateyev, called for volunteers to go into the reactor room and weld a new cooling system. The men would work in three-man shifts for five to ten minutes, wearing only raincoats and gas masks for protection.

The first volunteer stumbled out of the reactor room after only five minutes. He tore off his gas mask and vomited. Volunteers continued to go into the reactor, however, and eventually they succeeded in fixing the cooling pipe. The Soviet sub did not explode.

But the radiation had done its harm. The appearance of the men who had gone into the reactor changed. Skin reddened and swelled. Dots of blood appeared on foreheads and scalps. Within two hours, the sailors could not be recognized. Within days eight had died. Within two years, fourteen more eventually died of radiation poisoning.

Like radiation, evil is deadly to the body, soul, and spirit. Just as a raincoat and gas mask could not protect those Russian sailors from radiation, neither can intelligence or education, money or power protect us from the harmful effects of indulgences in evil. Safety can only be found in Jesus Christ and holy living.

Holiness, Occult, Reaping, Sowing
Rom. 6:23; Gal. 6:7–8

Date used _____ Place _____

Example   53

The power of a person's example is often unseen until years later. Writer Mike Lupica tells of the impact that great athletes of the past had on basketball star Grant Hill.

In a world of flashy young stars, National Basketball Association rookie Grant Hill is an oddity. He does not draw attention to himself with a big mouth or an act or jewelry or hair or dances or trash talk. He conducts himself with an elegance that seems more uncommon in sports than a solid collective-bargaining agreement.

"When I was young, I remember watching Julius Erving," he says. "The thing I liked best about Doctor J was that he carried himself with class. He never went out of his way to embarrass anybody. I feel like I come from a generation that has the wrong type of heroes. I never got to see Arthur Ashe play tennis, but I saw the way he lived his life after tennis. I always felt that was the type of person I should be looking up to because of his spirit. It's a matter of respect."

Heroes, Respect, Youth
2 Thess. 3:9; 1 Tim. 4:12

Date used _____ Place _____

Business consultant James M. Bleech of Jacksonville, Florida, surveyed 110 executives to find out what excuses they hear most from their employees.

Heading the list was "It's not my fault."

The second-place excuse was "It was someone else's fault."

Third, "Something else came up."

The fourth most often used excuse was "I didn't have time" followed by "We've never done it that way before."

Other excuses were "No one told me to do it," "I had too many interruptions," "If only my supervisor really understood," "I will get to it later," and "No one showed me how to do it."

Excuses don't impress anyone, least of all God.

Judgment, Ministry, Work
Matt. 25:14–30; Luke 14:16–24; Rom. 1:20

Date used _____ Place _____

When drivers explain their auto accidents, they can come up with some amazing explanations. Ann Landers gave these humorous examples from insurance reports provided to one insurance company.

"A pedestrian hit me and went under my car."

"The guy was all over the place. I had to swerve a number of times before I hit him."

"The accident occurred when I was attempting to bring my car out of a skid by steering into the other vehicle."

"As I approached the intersection, a stop sign suddenly appeared in a place where no stop sign had ever appeared before. I was unable to stop in time to avoid the accident."

"The telephone pole was approaching fast. I was attempting to swerve out of its path when it struck my front end."

"To avoid hitting the bumper of the car in front, I struck the pedestrian."

"An invisible car came out of nowhere, struck my vehicle and vanished."

"The pedestrian had no idea which direction to go, so I ran him over."

The excuses we try to give God sound just as lame.

Failure, Rationalization, Sin
Prov. 19:3; Luke 10:29; 14:15–24

Date used _____ Place _____

Extra Mile

Christian financial consultant and author Larry Burkett tells in *Business by the Book* about going the extra mile.

In 1984 he leased an office in a building that proved to be a nightmare. The foundation had not been properly constructed, and the office building was literally sinking several inches a year into the ground. After more than three years of putting up with assorted problems, including power failures and several weeks without water, Burkett moved his business to another location.

Two months later Burkett received a call from his former landlord who demanded that Burkett remodel and repaint his former office space. Burkett said no, feeling he had already been more than fair with the landlord, but the former landlord continued to call with his demands. Burkett consulted an attorney who agreed that Burkett had fulfilled his responsibility and should not do anything further. Burkett writes,

> The Lord used my oldest son to offer me some counsel. He reminded me that the man and his wife had lost their only child a few years earlier and still suffered from that tragedy. We had often commented that we would like to help them. . . . My son suggested that this might be an opportunity to go that extra mile the Lord suggested.
>
> As I considered that, I had to agree with his conclusion. We decided to commit several thousand dollars to restore a virtually nonusable building.

Going the extra mile doesn't usually make good business sense, but it makes great spiritual sense.

Business, Grace
Matt. 5:38–42

Date used _____ Place _____

Faith

In the October 1993 issue of *Life* magazine, a photo by Scott Threlkeld shows three teenage boys who have jumped from a thirty-foot-high cypress branch toward a dark Louisiana pond. Threlkeld evidently climbed the tree and shot from above the shirtless, soaring Huck Finns, for we look down on the boys and the pond.

There's something inspiring, even spiritual, about this picture.

The lanky boy on the right shows the least confidence, jumping feet first, knees bent and legs spread, ungainly arms flapping like a drunken stork about to make a crash landing.

The middle boy dives head first, arms spread stiffly straight and perpendicular, like the wings of a Piper Cub airplane. His head is slightly ducked and to the right, as if he were approaching the runway against a side wind. He is in a hurry to reach the water.

The third boy also dives head first but he isn't hurrying toward the tunnel-dark pond. He is floating. His head is up. His body is in a relaxed arch, both knees slightly bent, legs slightly apart. His arms are nonchalantly straight, hanging from his shoulders in an upside-down V. Poised and self-assured, as playful as an acrobat on the flying trapeze, he knows exactly where he is and, it appears, waits until the last moment to lift his arms, duck his head, and slip into the water.

No matter their kinesthetic sense or style, each of these three boys did a challenging thing: He took a scary leap.

Granted, high dives into country backwaters aren't always wise, but sometimes to follow God we must take a similar leap of faith. When we do, we will find that the kingdom of God is in the pond.

Fear, Ministry, Obedience, Risk, Service
Matt. 14:22–33; Heb. 11:8–10

Date used _____ Place _____

In *Christianity Today,* Philip Yancey writes:

I remember my first visit to Old Faithful in Yellowstone National Park. Rings of Japanese and German tourists surrounded the geyser, their video cameras trained like weapons on the famous hole in the ground. A large, digital clock stood beside the spot, predicting 24 minutes until the next eruption.

My wife and I passed the countdown in the dining room of Old Faithful Inn overlooking the geyser. When the digital clock reached one minute, we, along with every other diner, left our seats and rushed to the windows to see the big, wet event.

I noticed that immediately, as if on signal, a crew of busboys and waiters descended on the tables to refill water glasses and clear away dirty dishes. When the geyser went off, we tourists oohed and aahed and clicked our cameras; a few spontaneously applauded. But, glancing back over my shoulder, I saw that not a single waiter or busboy—not even those who had finished their chores—looked out the huge windows. Old Faithful, grown entirely too familiar, had lost its power to impress them.

Few things are more quickly taken for granted than God's faithfulness. But few things are more important. God's faithfulness deserves our untiring praise and wonder.

Familiarity, Thanksgiving, Wonder, Worship
Ps. 145; Luke 17:11–19; Heb. 10:23

Date used _____ Place _____

According to Reuters, one judge in London, England, awarded a divorce to a fifty-six-year-old woman apparently because her husband was a cheapskate. The woman's husband charged her $7.50 to repaint the living room of their London home. When his married daughter came to visit, he demanded that she pay eight cents to use the shower. He collected seventy-five cents a week from his family to pay for the electricity used when they watched television. When the couple was first married in 1947, he refused to take her on a honeymoon. He never gave her a birthday present.

In good English style the judge said that the man "had very peculiar ideas about family finances."

The divorce was the final nail in the coffin of a relationship that had died long, long before. Stinginess kills a relationship. Marriage and family life are based on unselfish giving. If you stop giving, you destroy love.

Giving, Husbands, Marriage, Money, Stinginess
Matt. 20:26–28; 2 Cor. 8:9; Eph. 5:25

Date used _____ Place _____

In an interview for *Today's Christian Woman,* writer and speaker Carol Kent says:

> One day when [my son] Jason was young, we were eating break-fast together. I had on an old pair of slacks and a fuzzy old sweater. He flashed his baby blues at me over his cereal bowl and said, "Mommy, you look so pretty today."
>
> I didn't even have makeup on! So I said, "Honey, why would you say I look pretty today? Normally I'm dressed up in a suit and high heels."
>
> And he said, "When you look like that, I know you're going some place; but when you look like this, I know you're all mine."

Nothing can replace the beauty of being together with those we love.

Beauty, Busyness, Love, Mothers, Priorities
Prov. 31:10–31; John 17:24

Date used _____ Place _____

Have you ever feared driving over a high bridge? If so, you're not alone. In fact, some people are so afraid of bridges that they will drive hours out of their way to avoid them. Others try to cross but have a panic attack in the middle of a bridge and can't go on. They block traffic.

Because of this the operators of some of the longest and highest spans in America now offer a driving service. On request, one of the bridge attendants will get behind the wheel and drive the car over the bridge.

In 1991 Michigan's Timid Motorist Program assisted 830 drivers across the Mackinac Bridge, which is five miles long and rises two hundred feet above the water.

At Maryland's Chesapeake Bay Bridge, which is over four miles long and rises two hundred feet above the water, authorities took the wheel and helped one thousand fearful motorists.

Bridges aren't the only things causing fear in people's hearts. In any terrifying situation the way to get over the paralysis of fear is to do like these motorists—turn the wheel over to someone else. Turn the situation over to God and then trust him. You have to cross that bridge, but you're not doing it alone, and God is the One in control.

Panic, Prayer, Trust
Ps. 56:3; 1 Peter 5:7

Date used _____ Place _____

Fear

On August 14, 1989, *Time* reported the sad story of a man from East Detroit who died of fear. He had taken a number of fur-trapping expeditions over the years and had been bitten by his share of ticks. Then he heard about Lyme disease, which is carried by deer ticks. He became obsessed with the fear that he had been bitten in the past by a tick with the disease and that he had passed the disease to his wife.

Doctors tested him and assured him he didn't have Lyme disease and that, even if he did, the disease was virtually impossible to transmit to his wife. But the man didn't believe the doctors. Paranoid, because of the disease, the man killed his wife and then himself.

The police found the man's mailbox jammed with material describing Lyme disease and a slip confirming a doctor's appointment for yet another Lyme-disease test.

Fear distorts a person's sense of reality. Fear consumes a person's energy and thoughts. Fear controls.

Faith, Trust, Worry
Mark 4:40; John 14:27

Date used _____ Place _____

On the prairies of the Midwest, a grass fire can be a good thing.

"To ask whether a prairie needs fire is to wonder whether it needs water," says writer Cindy Schreuder. "Burns stimulate the growth of grasses and forbs, return nutrients to the soil, expose seed beds to the sun and suppress invading trees and shrubs."

During the 1960s, as people in the prairie restoration movement saw the benefits of a regular prairie fire, the practice of intentionally setting such fires became widespread. Schreuder describes one such fire:

> Pushed forward by the wind, the flames raced across the prairie. Thick, dead grass stalks wavered for just a moment before buckling and falling into flames. . . .
>
> Nineteenth-century settlers spoke of the violence of the burns, their noise, heat, power and attraction. They are reactions modern-day scientists share. "A prairie burning is something like a great thunderstorm—you experience the raw power of nature," said [Stephen Packard, science director for the Nature Conservancy, Illinois]. "After you've burned it off, nothing is left. It's so pure. Every leaf that emerges is new and shiny and wet. Every flower petal is perfect. It reminds you of being young."

In the same way, God's consuming fire brings new life when we willingly let him burn the fields of our hearts.

Altar, Cleansing, Holiness, Purging, Repentance, Revival, Sacrifice
Mal. 3:3; Heb. 12:29; James 4:6–10; 1 Peter 4:17

Date used _____ Place _____

Mountain goats live in a precarious environment. One wrong move and they can fall to their deaths. Young mountain goats can be in special danger because of their playfulness.

Douglas Chadwick in *National Geographic* writes that the kids of mountain goats are "born to romp—and leap, twist, skip, prance. . . . High spirits and wandering attention can be fatal for young goats. Fortunately, nannies dote on their offspring, tending them from the downhill side to block falls. . . ."

What a beautiful image for how mature Christians should care for new believers. New Christians will stumble and fall on occasion—that is certain—so we must tend them from the downhill side, ready to block them when they fall. Tending from the downhill side means staying in regular communication.

Discipleship, Growth
Gal. 6:1

Date used _____ Place _____

In *Restoring Your Spiritual Passion*, Gordon MacDonald writes:

One memory that burns deep within is that of a plane flight on which I was headed toward a meeting that would determine a major decision in my ministry. I knew I was in desperate need of a spiritual passion that would provide wisdom and submission to God's purposes. But the passion was missing because I was steeped in resentment toward a colleague.

For days I had tried everything to rid myself of vindictive thoughts toward that person. But, try as I might, I would even wake in the night, thinking of ways to subtly get back at him. I wanted to embarrass him for what he had done, to damage his credibility before his peers. My resentment was beginning to dominate me, and on that plane trip I came to a realization of how bad things really were. . . .

As the plane entered the landing pattern, I found myself crying silently to God for power both to forgive and to experience liberation from my poisoned spirit. Suddenly it was as if an invisible knife cut a hole in my chest, and I literally felt a thick substance oozing from within. Moments later I felt as if I'd been flushed out. I'd lost negative spiritual weight, the kind I needed to lose: I was free. I fairly bounced off that plane and soon entered a meeting that did in fact change the entire direction of my life.

Spiritual passion cannot coexist with resentments. The Scriptures are clear. The unforgiving spirit saps the energy that causes Christian growth and effectiveness.

Anger, Prayer, Resentment, Thoughts
Matt. 6:12; Eph. 4:30–32

Date used _____ Place _____

Used by permission of the publisher.

In *The Grace Awakening,* Charles Swindoll recalls the sense of freedom he had when as a teenager he first received his driver's license. His dad rewarded him.

"Tell you what, son . . . you can have the car for two hours, all on your own." Only four words, but how wonderful: "All on your own."

I thanked him. . . . My pulse rate must have shot up to 180 as I backed out of the driveway and roared off. While cruising along "all on my own," I began to think wild stuff—like, *This car can probably do 100 miles an hour. I could go to Galveston and back twice in two hours if I averaged 100 miles an hour. I can fly down the Gulf Freeway and even run a few lights. After all, nobody's here to say "Don't!"* We're talking dangerous, crazy thoughts! But you know what? I didn't do any of them. I don't believe I drove above the speed limit. In fact, I distinctly remember turning into the driveway early. . . . I had my dad's car all to myself with a full gas tank in a context of total privacy and freedom, but I didn't go crazy. Why? My relationship with my dad and my grandad was so strong that I couldn't, even though I had a license and nobody was in the car to restrain me. Over a period of time, there had developed a sense of trust, a deep love relationship that held me in restraint.

In the same way, our love for Christ keeps us from abusing the freedom he gives us.

Fathers, Love, Sin, Trust
Gal. 5; 1 Peter 2:16

Date used _____ Place _____

André-François Raffray, a retired lawyer in Arles, France, made what any reasonable businessman would say was a sound financial decision. According to the *Chicago Tribune*, for a five-hundred-dollar-a-month annuity, he bought the rights to take over an apartment in Arles, France, on the death of its current resident. The woman living in the apartment was Jeanne Calment, age ninety. Actuarial tables predicting the mathematical probabilities of Jeanne Calment's life span were clearly on the lawyer's side.

Thirty years later and $180,000 poorer, Raffray had still not moved into the apartment. On Tuesday, February 21, 1995, Jeanne Calment celebrated her 120th birthday. She was verifiably the oldest person in the world. Each year on her birthday she sends Raffray a card that jokingly says, "Sorry I am still alive."

How little control we humans have of the future!

Aging, Control, Death, Foreknowledge, Sovereignty of God
Ps. 31:15; Isa. 41:21–27; Acts 2:23; 1 Peter 1:2

Date used _____ Place _____

In *Honest to God,* Bill Hybels writes:

Recently my brother and I spent a lunch hour discussing the mark our dad left on our lives. . . .

Dan and I reminisced about the times we had sailed with him on Lake Michigan. We remembered violent storms with fifty-mile-an-hour winds. All the other sailors would dash for the harbor, but Dad would smile from ear to ear and say, "Let's head out farther!"

We talked about the tough business decisions we had seen him make. We winced when we remembered his firm hand of discipline that blocked our rebellious streaks. We never doubted it. Dad was strong, tough, and thoroughly masculine.

Yet for twenty-five years he spent nearly every Sunday afternoon standing in front of a hundred mentally retarded women at the state mental hospital. Gently and patiently he led them in a song service. Few of them could even sing, but he didn't care. He knew it made them feel loved. Afterward he stood by the door while each of those disheveled, broken women planted kisses on his cheek. As little guys, Dan and I had the unspeakable privilege of watching our six-foot-three, two-hundred-twenty-pound, thoroughly masculine dad treat these forgotten women with a gentleness that marked us.

Fathers, Love, Masculinity, Strength
Matt. 11:29; Eph. 4:2

Date used _____ Place _____

According to the Associated Press, in October 1994, Harvard University Law School announced it had just received the largest cash gift ever given to a law school: a cool thirteen million dollars.

The donors were Gustave and Rita Hauser. What was it that inspired such generosity? Romance and gratitude. Back in 1955 Gustave and Rita met at the law school. The day after final exams in 1956, they married. They went on to become highly successful in business. Hauser, who is chairman and CEO of Hauser Communications and formerly head of the Warner Bros. cable unit, was one of the pioneers of cable television and a developer of the Nickelodeon channel. Gustave Hauser never did practice law. It seems his deep gratitude to Harvard was because of its role as matchmaker. Said Hauser at a ceremony announcing the donation, "The school had a unique role in bringing us together."

When we are given much—and are mature enough to be grateful—we naturally want to give much. God gave us his only Son, Jesus Christ. It is no wonder, then, that we find great joy in giving back to God our time, energy, abilities, and money. We owe God everything.

Devotion, Generosity, Gratitude, Love, Offering, Sacrifice
Matt. 10:8; 2 Cor. 5:14–15; Gal. 2:20

Date used _____ Place _____

In *Leadership*, pastor and author Stu Weber writes:

My youngest son is the third of three boys. The first two are high-powered; the third is not any less high-powered, but he's the third out of three. By the time you've had a brother who's All-Conference this and another brother who's All-Conference that, there's not much left for you to do.

As a father, I worried about our caboose. He is the most sensitive of the three. To encourage him, I spent a lot of time with him in the outdoors—camping, hunting, fishing. Anybody who has spent time in the outdoors knows that a pocketknife is essential gear—the man with the best blade gets the job done. So, whenever you're setting up camp, you're always looking for the knife.

My son Ryan had a pocketknife that became his identity. His older brothers always had to ask him to use the knife as we were setting up camp. That became his status in the tribe. He was the man with the blade.

My birthday came around one year, and my family was planning a party for me. Earlier in the afternoon my youngest walked into my office at home where I was studying. At first I didn't hear him; I felt him—I could sense his presence—and I turned around.

He had chosen this moment because he wanted to give me a birthday present but not at the birthday party. He wanted it to be just me and him. He handed me a present, and I opened it—it was his knife.

When we want to express our love for God, we also delight in giving him what is most important to us.

Children, Fathers, Intimacy, Love for God
Num. 18:29; John 3:16; 12:1–8

Date used _____ Place _____

According to *USA Today,* on Wednesday, November 23, 1994, a couple named Sandy and Theresa boarded TWA flight 265 in New York to fly to Orlando and see Disney World. Theresa was almost seven months pregnant. Thirty minutes into the flight, Theresa doubled over in pain and began bleeding. Flight attendants announced that they needed a doctor, and a Long Island internist volunteered.

Theresa soon gave birth to a boy. But the baby was in trouble. The umbilical cord was wrapped tightly around his neck, and he wasn't breathing. His face was blue.

Two paramedics rushed forward to help, one of whom specialized in infant respiratory procedures. He asked if anyone had a straw, which he wanted to use to suction fluid from the baby's lungs. The plane did not stock straws, but a flight attendant remembered having a straw left over from a juice box she had brought on board the plane. The paramedic inserted the straw in the baby's lungs as the internist administered CPR. The internist asked for something he could use to tie off the umbilical cord. A passenger offered a shoelace.

Four minutes of terror passed. Then the little baby whimpered. Soon the crew was able to joyfully announce that it was a boy, and everyone on board cheered and clapped.

The parents gave the little boy the name Matthew. Matthew means "Godsent." The people on board the plane "were all godsends," the father said.

Indeed, God had met the need through people who gave what they had and did what they could. God usually meets needs through people.

Body of Christ, Church, Needs, Spiritual gifts, Teamwork
Rom. 12:3–8; 1 Cor. 12; 2 Cor. 8–9

Date used _____ Place _____

A Tampa chiropractor had paid alimony to his former wife for a long time. In 1994 he came to his final alimony payment of $182. He didn't just want to send his money; he wanted to send a message. So in large scale he drew a check on the back of a pinstripe shirt. On the memo line of his shirt-check, he wrote, "Here it is—the shirt off my back!" The bank cashed it.

When there is no love, giving leads to bitterness.

Bitterness, Love for God, Money, Resentment
2 Cor. 9:7

Date used _____ Place _____

Leave it to a children's book to help us see how big our universe is. In a book entitled *Is a Blue Whale the Biggest Thing There Is?* Robert Wells takes us from a size we can grasp to one we can't.

The largest animal on earth is the blue whale. Just the flippers on its tail are bigger than most animals on earth.

But a blue whale isn't anywhere near as big as a mountain. If you put one hundred blue whales in a huge jar, you could put millions of whale jars inside a hollowed-out Mount Everest.

But Mount Everest isn't anywhere near as big as the earth. If you stacked one hundred Mount Everests on top of one another, it would be just a whisker on the face of the earth.

And the earth isn't anywhere near as big as the sun. You could fit one million earths inside of the sun.

But the sun, which is a medium-size star, isn't anywhere near as big as a red supergiant star called Antares. Fifty million of our suns could fit inside of Antares.

But Antares isn't anywhere near as big as the Milky Way galaxy. Billions of stars, including supergiants like Antares, as well as countless comets and asteroids, make up the Milky Way galaxy.

But the Milky Way galaxy isn't anywhere near as big as the universe. There are *billions* of other *galaxies* in the universe.

And yet, filled with billions of galaxies, the universe is almost totally empty. The distances from one galaxy to another are beyond our imagination.

And the Creator of this universe is God, who with a Word spoke it all into being, who is present everywhere in this universe and beyond, who upholds it all with his mighty power. Great is our God and greatly to be praised!

Creation, Omnipresence, Power of God
Gen. 1; Ps. 19:1–6; Isa. 40:18–26; John 1:1–3

Date used _____ Place _____

On Saturday, September 18, 1982, the U.S. government released the results of a sad investigation. The government determined that an army soldier stationed in Korea had been a defector to the Communists. According to the investigation, on August 28, 1982, this twenty-year-old private willingly crossed the Korean Demilitarized Zone into North Korea "for motives that are not known." His fellow American soldiers pleaded with him to turn back, but he did not respond.

The day after the findings were released, the parents of the young man held a press conference on the lawn of their St. Louis home. Wiping tears from his eyes, the father said that they had accepted the fact that their son was indeed a defector. "He has lost his credibility in this country, even with me," said the man. But then he showed the heart of a father. "I still love my son," he said, "and want him back."

God is like this father. You may have turned away from him, but if you will come back, the door is open, and the light is on. Come home, says the Father. Please come home.

Forgiveness, Love of God, Mercy
Luke 15:11–24; John 3:16; Rom. 5:8; Rev. 22:17

Date used _____ Place _____

Goodness 75

Bodie Thoene, coauthor of bestselling Christian fiction such as the *Zion Chronicles,* once worked for John Wayne as a script writer. In *Today's Christian Woman*, Thoene tells how that opportunity came about.

By the time I was nineteen, I was commuting to Los Angeles and doing feature articles on different stunt men and other film personalities for magazines. Four years later, an article I co-wrote with John Wayne's stuntman won the attention of the Duke himself. One day he called and invited [my husband,] Brock, and me to come to his house. He talked to us as if we were friends, showing keen interest in us as individuals. From that day on, I began writing for his film company, Batjac Productions. Brock helped me with the historical research.

We were awestruck. Here was this man who had been in film for fifty years and he takes a young couple with small children under his wing! Once I asked him, "Why are you doing this? You're so good to us."

He replied, "Because somebody did it for me."

Goodness doesn't originate with us. We receive, and then we give. God is good to all, enabling all to be good to others.

Generosity, Giving
Matt. 5:43–48; 10:8; 1 John 4:19

Date used _____ Place _____

One of the great heartbreaks of the 1988 Winter Olympics was the story of speed skater Dan Jansen. Just hours before his race he received the news that his sister, who had been fighting leukemia for more than a year, had just died. Bearing the weight of his sorrow, Dan laced on his skates to race for his sister. When the gun sounded, he sprinted from the starting line, only to slip and fall in the first turn. Four days later, in the 1,000-meter race, he fell again. The whole country mourned with him.

Many Americans sent Dan letters of consolation. According to *Sports Illustrated*, not long after returning home, Jansen received a letter from Mark Arrowood, a disabled thirty-year-old from Doylestown, Pennsylvania. Mark wrote:

> Dear Dan, I watched you on TV. I'm sorry that you fell 2 times. I am in Special Olympics. I won a gold medal at Pa. State Summer Olympics right after my Dad died seven years ago. . . . Before we start the games we have a saying that goes like this. "Let me win but if I can't win let me be brave in the attempt." . . . I want to share one of my gold medals with you because I don't like to see you not get one. Try again in four more years.

Inside the envelope, Dan Jansen found a gold medal that Mark Arrowood had won in a track-and-field event.

Those who share their blessings are the greatest champions of all. Goodness is greatness.

Giving, Kindness, Love, Sharing
Acts 2:44–45; Gal. 5:22–23; 2 Peter 1:5–8

Date used _____ Place _____

In *Robins Reader,* Frank W. Mann Jr. writes:

An enlightening pastime is to make a list of favorite things that impact the senses. . . . It sharpens our appreciation of these golden moments in time.

For example, one person's list of ten favorite sounds: a distant train whistle; a mother talking to her new baby; the scrunch of leaves on a bright autumn day; seagulls crying; a hound baying in the woods at night; the absolute silence of a mountain lake at sunset; a crackling fire on a bitter day; a stadium crowd singing the national anthem; the screech of an airplane's tires as they touch down; his wife's voice at morning.

God gave us our five senses and then he filled his creation with pleasures for each sense. God is exceedingly good.

Pleasure, Thanksgiving
Ps. 34:8; Prov. 20:12; 1 Tim. 4:4

Date used _____ Place _____

Phil Knight founded the Nike shoe company in 1972, and in less than two decades it became one of the strongest and most well-recognized companies in the world. Unique and unforgettable advertising is what powered its phenomenal corporate growth.

When you think of classic Nike advertising, you think of superstar athletes—Michael Jordan, Charles Barkley, and Bo Jackson—and you think of the phrase "Just Do It." You think of Spike Lee muttering about Michael Jordan, "It's gotta be the shoes" or Charles Barkley announcing, "Just because I can dunk a basketball doesn't mean I should raise your kids."

In 1994 the Cannes International Advertising Festival recognized the consistent creativity and impact of Nike advertising by naming Nike advertiser of the year.

That is unimaginable to anyone who knew how Nike CEO Phil Knight felt about advertising back in 1981. That's when Phil Knight first hired a new ad agency. When Knight met with the ad agency's president, Knight told him to his face, "I hate advertising."

The greatest advertiser in the world once hated advertising! The company made by advertising started its relationship with its ad agency skeptical and dubious.

In the same way, many people who once hated the gospel of Jesus Christ now love that gospel. It has brought them all the good they now enjoy.

Change, Evangelism, Repentance
Mark 1:15; John 9:25; Rom. 1:16

Date used _____ Place _____

In *World Vision*, writer Tony Campolo tells of taking an airplane from California to Philadelphia one stormy night. It was late, but when the man in the next seat learned that Campolo was a Christian, he wanted to talk. "I believe that going to heaven is like going to Philadelphia," the man said. You can get there by airplane, by train, by bus, by automobile. There are many ways to get to Philadelphia. Campolo writes:

As we started descending into Philadelphia, the place was fogged in. The wind was blowing, the rain was beating on the plane, and everyone looked nervous and tight. As we were circling in the fog, I turned to the theological expert on my right. "I'm certainly glad the pilot doesn't agree with your theology," I said.

"What do you mean?" he asked.

"The people in the control booth are giving instructions to the pilot: 'Coming north by northwest, three degrees, you're on beam you're on beam, don't deviate from beam.' I'm glad the pilot's not saying, 'There are many ways into the airport. There are many approaches we can take.' I'm glad he is saying, 'There's only one way we can land this plane, and I'm going to stay with it.'"

There is only one way to God, and that is through Jesus Christ.

Evangelism, Salvation
John 14:6; Acts 4:12; 1 John 5:12

Date used _____ Place _____

Gospel

In *The Whisper Test,* Mary Ann Bird writes:

I grew up knowing I was different, and I hated it. I was born with a cleft palate, and when I started school, my classmates made it clear to me how I looked to others: a little girl with a misshapen lip, crooked nose, lopsided teeth, and garbled speech.

When schoolmates asked, "What happened to your lip?" I'd tell them I'd fallen and cut it on a piece of glass. Somehow it seemed more acceptable to have suffered an accident than to have been born different. I was convinced that no one outside my family could love me.

There was, however, a teacher in the second grade that we all adored—Mrs. Leonard by name. She was short, round, happy—a sparkling lady.

Annually we had a hearing test. . . .

Mrs. Leonard gave the test to everyone in the class, and finally it was my turn. I knew from past years that as we stood against the door and covered one ear, the teacher sitting at her desk would whisper something, and we would have to repeat it back—things like "The sky is blue" or "Do you have new shoes?" I waited there for those words that God must have put into her mouth, those seven words that changed my life. Mrs. Leonard said, in her whisper, "I wish you were my little girl."

God says to every person deformed by sin, "I wish you were my son" or "I wish you were my daughter."

Acceptance, Grace, Love of God, Mercy, Sin
Rom. 5:8; Eph. 2:1–5

Date used _____ Place _____

Who can forget the 1994 tabloid headline "Killer Bug Ate My Face"? Although the reporting was sensational, the stories were based on seven real cases of invasive strep A bacteria in Gloucestershire, England.

When invasive strep A (which is not the same as strep throat) takes hold in a victim's body, necrotizing fasciitis can begin, which means that the flesh starts to die at an incredible rate of several inches per hour. Meanwhile toxic shock can set in, shutting down organs and causing death.

Geoffrey Cowley describes scientifically what happens after the deadly microbes take hold in a victim's body.

> The bacteria then multiply rapidly, producing toxins in the process. For three days, the patient may suffer swollen lymph nodes, a rising fever and excruciating pain at the site of infection. Penicillin can stop the attack at this stage, but by day four, infected tissues start dying. Bacteria soon saturate the bloodstream, destroying muscles and organs and sending the body into shock. Death can follow within hours. . . . Invasive strep is rare, but it's also unforgiving.

Is there any counterpart to the strep A bacteria in the body of Christ? Yes. Nothing can so quickly eat the flesh of the church as sins of the tongue: gossip, slander, criticism of leaders, and bad reports.

Body of Christ, Grumbling, Tongue
Prov. 16:28; Eph. 4:29–31; James 3:5–7; 5:9

Date used _____ Place _____

In the early nineties, the leaning Tower of Pisa began to lean too far. Seeing that the 180-foot-high tower would soon become dangerous, engineers designed a system to salvage the twelfth-century landmark by holding the lean constant.

First the engineers injected super cold liquid nitrogen into the ground to freeze it and thereby minimize dangerous ground vibrations during the work that followed. Then they plan to install cables to pull the structure more upright. Engineers hope that the underground cable network will pull the tower toward center by at least an inch. The work is to be completed in 1996.

Left to itself, our world resembles the leaning Tower of Pisa: tilting and heading to catastrophe. To prevent total anarchy, God establishes governments to maintain order. Governments and their laws function like the steel cables that will hold the leaning tower. The tower still leans. It's not perfect. But the cables prevent total destruction.

Authority, Law, Rulers, Submission, Taxes
Rom. 13:1–7; 1 Peter 2:13–17

Date used _____ Place _____

In *The Christian Reader,* Paul Francisco writes:

When I was a child, our church celebrated the Lord's Supper every first Sunday of the month. At that service, the offering plates were passed twice: before the sermon for regular offerings, and just prior to Communion for benevolences. My family always gave to both, but they passed a dime to me to put in only the regular offering.

One Communion Sunday when I was nine, my mother, for the first time, gave me a dime for the benevolent offering also. A little later when the folks in our pew rose to go to the Communion rail, I got up also. "You can't take Communion yet," Mother told me.

"Why not?" I said. "I paid for it!"

This child's humorous story shows a very adult attitude. We may think we can earn God's salvation.

Communion, Faith, Jesus Christ, Salvation, Works
Rom. 3:21–25; Eph. 2:8–9

Date used _____ Place _____

According to the *Chicago Tribune*, in the summer of 1994, Marcio da Silva, a love-struck Brazilian artist, was distraught over the breakup of a four-year relationship with his girlfriend, Katia de Nascimento. He tried to win back her love by a gesture of great devotion. He walked on his knees for nine miles. With pieces of car tires tied to his kneecaps, the twenty-one-year-old man shuffled along for fourteen hours before he reached her home in Santos, Brazil. He was cheered on by motorists and passersby, but when he reached the end of his marathon of love thoroughly exhausted, the nineteen-year-old woman of his dreams was not impressed. She had intentionally left her home to avoid seeing him.

Some people try similar acts of devotion to impress God and earn salvation. Like Katia de Nascimento, God is not impressed. The only thing that brings the forgiveness of sin is faith in Jesus Christ, not sacrificial deeds.

Faith, Gospel, Sacrifice, Salvation, Works
Rom. 10:1–4; Eph. 2:8–9

Date used _____ Place _____

Grace

Pilot William Langewiesche writes in *Atlantic Monthly:*

> In clouds or on black nights, when they cannot see outside, pilots keep their wings level by watching an artificial horizon on the instrument panel. The artificial horizon is a gyroscopically steadied line, which stays level with the earth's surface.

Langewiesche says that pilots sometimes become confused about what the instruments are telling them. He says:

> As turbulence tilts the airplane to the left, the pilots, tilting with it, notice the artificial horizon line dropping to the right. Reacting instinctively to the indication of motion, they sometimes try to raise the line as if it were a wing. The result of such a reversal is murderous. Pilots steer to the left just when they should steer to the right, and then in confusion they steer harder. While cruising calmly inside clouds, I have had student pilots suddenly try to flip the airplane upside down.

The same kind of disorientation can happen when we seek God's acceptance. When we see how far short we fall of God's will, we can try harder and harder to be good, hoping that if we become almost perfect, God will accept us. But that's precisely the opposite of what we need to do. Instead we should trust in God's grace.

Legalism, Righteousness, Salvation, Trust, Works
Rom. 10:2–4; Gal. 5:1–6; Eph. 2:8–9

Date used _____ Place _____

In *The Grace Awakening,* Charles Swindoll writes:

I vividly remember my last spanking. It was on my thirteenth birthday, as a matter of fact. Having just broken into the sophisticated ranks of the teen world, I thought I was something on a stick. My father wasn't nearly as impressed as I was with my great importance and new-found independence. I was lying on my bed. He was outside the window on a muggy October afternoon in Houston, weeding the garden. He said, "Charles, come out and help me weed the garden." I said something like: "No . . . it's my birthday, remember?" My tone was sassy and my deliberate lack of respect was eloquent. I knew better than to disobey my dad, but after all, I was the ripe old age of thirteen. He set a new 100-meter record that autumn afternoon. He was in the house and all over me like white on rice, spanking me all the way out to the garden. As I recall, I weeded until the moonlight was shining on the pansies.

That same night he took me out to a surprise dinner. He gave me what I deserved earlier. Later he gave me what I did not deserve. The birthday dinner was grace.

Child rearing, Discipline, Fathers, Obedience
Eph. 2:8–9; Heb. 12:5–11

Date used _____ Place _____

The Grace Awakening, Charles Swindoll, 1990, Word, Dallas, Texas. All rights reserved.
Used by permission.

Guilt 87

For some time the *Chicago Tribune Magazine* ran a column about people's jobs. A writer would interview an average cop or baker or legal secretary about what it was like to do his or her work. One column told the story of a man named Neil Boyle who read depositions in jury trials. Boyle told of one crazy lawsuit he had seen.

A hospital-supply corporation falsified its annual reports so that the shareholders thought it was doing better financially than it was. An auditing firm came in, but the company manipulated its inventory, moving the same goods to whatever warehouse the firm was inspecting. When the fraud was finally discovered, the corporation sued the auditing firm for not catching them! The auditing firm eventually won, but it took 11 years.

Some people will never acknowledge their guilt.

Blame, Confession, Deception, Justice
1 John 1:8–10

Date used _____ Place _____

According to *Time* magazine, in 1970 Katherine Power, a student at Brandeis University in Boston, was a leader of the radical National Student Strike Force. She and several others planned to raise money to buy arms for the Black Panthers by robbing a bank.

Kathy drove the getaway car. But the robbery went awry. A silent alarm was quickly answered by patrolman Walter Schroeder. Shots were fired by one of Kathy's accomplices, and patrolman Schroeder was killed.

That night Kathy began what would be twenty-three years of life on the lam. Listed as armed and "very dangerous," she was on the FBI's most-wanted list.

In the late 1970s, Power moved to Oregon. There she assumed the name Alice Metzinger, settled down, started a new life in the restaurant business, bought a house, gave birth to her son, and married. She was an active part of the community and seemingly had every reason to be at peace.

But at age forty-four Kathy Power was desperately tired, tormented by guilt, and chronically depressed. Finally Kathy did the only thing she felt could end her agony. In September 1993 she turned herself in to Boston police. She explained why this was so important: "I am now learning to live with openness and truth," she said, "rather than shame and hiddenness."

Shame and guilt are feelings from which you cannot run and cannot hide. Freedom comes only by facing up to the truth—with people and with God.

Confession, Depression, Shame, Truth
Heb. 10:22; James 5:16; 1 John 1:9

Date used _____ Place _____

Hardness 89

Cardiologists are hunting for a way to clear arteries clogged by plaque. They've tried using lasers to burn through the plaque. They've experimented with rotating burrs to grind away the plaque. They've even tried using rotating knives to cut away plaque. None of these methods have succeeded.

At the annual meeting of the American Heart Association in 1993, researchers reported on another experimental device that would work like a tiny jackhammer inside the arteries. Writer Jon Van says the device is inserted into the coronary arteries via a tiny wire called a catheter. There it emits low-frequency, ultrasound energy, vibrating the jackhammer-like tip of the probe at 19,500 times a second, about one-thousandth of an inch back and forth each time. After the jackhammer has done its work, a balloon is inserted into the narrowed artery and expanded to open the artery.

In twenty-nine test cases, the jackhammer seemed to accomplish something the other methods could not. It broke down the calcium and gristle in the hard plaque without harming the soft walls of the artery.

Hardening of the arteries is the enemy of the heart. A dangerous hardness can also develop in our spiritual lives, a hardness that constricts the life-giving love of God in our lives. If your heart has been hardened, there is no better "jackhammer" than to humble yourself before the Lord.

Anger, Heart, Humility, Prayer, Repentance
Eph. 4:17–19; Heb. 3:13; 1 Peter 5:6

Date used _____ Place _____

Hatred of Evil

In May 1994 the Associated Press carried a story about one person's unusual war on sin. At the public library in Coquille, Oregon, library workers discovered at least a dozen books in which entire pages had been blanked out by a patron wielding white correction fluid. The unknown, self-appointed censor painted over naughty phrases and sexually explicit passages. "They've marked everything from love-swept romances to best sellers," said librarian Molly DePlois.

While conducting a war with white-out is probably not what God had in mind, Scripture *does* call us to hate what is evil.

Evil, Holiness, Purity, World
Rom. 12:9; James 1:27

Date used _____ Place _____

In his book *When You're All Out of Noodles*, Ken Jones writes about a lesson he learned one day at the office.

> [When I walked into my office,] I noticed something I had never seen before. It was round, about the size of a dessert plate, and plugged into the wall, giving out a constant noise. It wasn't a loud noise, just constant. *What in the world is that thing?* I thought as I stopped to stare.
>
> I finally asked the receptionist about it. She said, "It's an ambient noise generator. If it's too quiet in here, we can distinguish the voices in the counseling offices, and we want to protect their privacy. So we bought the noise generator to cover the voices."
>
> Her explanation made perfect sense to me, but didn't it have to be louder to mask the conversations, I asked. "No," she said. "The constancy of the sound tricks the ear so that what is being said can't be distinguished."
>
> *Interesting*, I thought. *Very interesting.* One kind of noise to cover the sound of another. It made me think and pray.
>
> *No wonder, Lord. No wonder I strain to hear what you have to say to me. . . . The constancy of sound—little noises, soft, inward, ambient thoughts and fears and attitudes—tricks the ears of my inner man and masks your still, small voice.*

God isn't silent. We just have trouble hearing him.

Listening, Silence, Solitude, Spiritual discernment, Spiritual disciplines
1 Kings 19:9–13; Ps. 46:10

Date used _____ Place _____

Dave Dravecky pitched for the San Francisco Giants in the 1980s. In 1988 doctors discovered a tumor in his pitching arm. In 1991 Dravecky's arm finally had to be amputated.

In *When You Can't Come Back,* Dave Dravecky writes about his sense of loss.

> I miss doing things with my own two hands, and—of course—I really miss baseball. There is a scene in the movie *Field of Dreams* where Shoeless Joe Jackson—one of the eight White Sox players banned from baseball for conspiring to lose the 1919 World Series—said, "Getting thrown out of baseball was like having part of me amputated. I'd wake up at night with the smell of the ballpark in my nose, the cool of the grass on my feet. Man, I did love this game. I'd have played for food money. It was a game. The sounds, the smells. I'd have played for nuthin'."

Dravecky comments, "That scene had a powerful effect on me. I missed those feelings too. The feel of stitched seams as you cradle a new ball in your hand. The smell of seasoned leather as you bring the glove to your face. The sound of a bat cracking out a base hit. I'd have played for food money. I'd have played for nuthin'."

How painful it is to lose what we love. Unfortunately in this fallen world, our lives are touched by loss over and over again. God wants us to enjoy what we love for all eternity, to never experience loss. That is the promise of heaven.

Eternal, Loss, Temporal, World
Matt. 6:19–21; 10:37–39; 16:23–27; 2 Cor. 4:16–18; Rev. 21:1–5

Date used _____ Place _____

Heaven

In *Six Hours One Friday,* Max Lucado wrote of a friend named Joy who taught a Sunday school class in an underprivileged area. Joy had in her class a timid, nine-year-old girl named Barbara. Max writes:

[Barbara's] difficult home life had left her afraid and insecure. For the weeks that my friend was teaching the class, Barbara never spoke. Never. While the other children talked, she sat. While the others sang, she was silent. While the others giggled, she was quiet.

Always present. Always listening. Always speechless.

Until the day Joy gave a class on heaven. Joy talked about seeing God. She talked about tearless eyes and deathless lives.

Barbara was fascinated. She wouldn't release Joy from her stare. She listened with hunger. Then she raised her hand. "Mrs. Joy?"

Joy was stunned. Barbara had never asked a question. "Yes, Barbara?"

"Is heaven for girls like me?"

Barbara couldn't be more qualified.

> Children, Hope
> Matt. 19:14; Eph. 1:11–14

Date used _____ Place _____

It was to be a majestic evening. On Friday, October 18, 1991, the world-class Chicago Symphony presented the final concert in its year-long celebration of the symphony's one hundredth year. For the first time in United States symphony history, the present conductor and two former conductors of an orchestra stood on the same stage: Rafael Kubelik, Georg Solti, and Daniel Barenboim. At a centenary celebration dinner before the concert, patrons had received souvenir clocks as gifts. As Daniel Barenboim sat down at the piano and Georg Solti lifted his baton to begin Tchaikovsky's First Piano Concerto, a great sense of drama filled Chicago's historic Orchestra Hall. And the beauty of the music took over.

A few minutes later, however, at 9:15 P.M., the music began to unravel. Out in the auditorium a little beep sounded. Then another, and another. Little beeps were sounding everywhere. Barenboim and the symphony plowed ahead, but everyone was distracted and the music suffered.

Finally, after the first movement ended, Henry Fogel, the executive director of the symphony, walked on stage to explain what had happened. The manufacturer of the souvenir clocks presented at the preconcert dinner had set the alarms to go off at 9:15.

Now there was only one way to get on with the concert. Fogel asked everyone who had one of the clocks to check them in with an usher.

Trivial things have terrible power to disrupt—or even make a farce—of what is important.

Distractions, Eternal, Materialism, Priorities, Temporal, Values
Luke 8:14; Phil. 3:7–8; Heb. 12:1

Date used _____ Place _____

According to writer Lisa Belcher-Hamilton, Fred Rogers, of the television program *Mister Rogers' Neighborhood,* took courses on how to preach during his time in seminary. Said Rogers:

> Years ago my wife and I were worshiping in a little church with friends of ours. We were on vacation, and I was in the middle of my homiletics course at the time.
>
> During the sermon I kept ticking off every mistake I thought the preacher—he must have been eighty years old—was making. When this interminable sermon finally ended, I turned to one of my friends, intending to say something critical about the sermon. I stopped myself when I saw the tears running down her face.
>
> She whispered to me, "He said exactly what I needed to hear." That was really a seminal experience for me. I was judging and she was needing, and the Holy Spirit responded to need, not judgment.

Although we must always give ministry our best effort, we must never forget that the Holy Spirit can work through even the most faulty instrument.

Criticism, Judging, Ministry, Preaching
Matt. 7:1–2; Eph. 4:29–32

Date used _____ Place _____

In *Flying Closer to the Flame*, Charles Swindoll writes:

Some years ago my phone rang in the middle of the day on a Friday. It was someone from our older daughter's school telling me that Charissa had been in an accident. She had been practicing a pyramid formation with her cheerleading squad when someone at the bottom slipped, causing the whole human pyramid to collapse. Charissa had been at the top and, consequently, fell the farthest, hitting the back of her head with a sharp jolt. Her legs and arms had gone numb, and she was unable to move even her fingers. After notifying the paramedics, the school official had called me.

My wife, Cynthia, was away at the time, so I raced to the school alone, not knowing what I'd find or how serious our daughter had been injured. En route, I prayed aloud. I called out to the Lord like a child trapped in an empty well. I told Him I would need Him for several things: to touch my daughter, to give me strength, to provide skill and wisdom to the paramedics. Tears were near the surface, so I asked Him to calm me, to restrain the growing sense of panic within me.

As I drove and prayed, I sensed the most incredible realization of God's presence. It was almost eerie. The pulse that had been thumping in my throat returned to normal. When I reached the school parking lot, even the swirling red and blue lights atop the emergency vehicle didn't faze my sense of calm.

I ran to where the crowd had gathered. By that time the paramedics had Charissa wrapped tightly on a stretcher, her neck in a brace. I knelt beside her, kissed her on the forehead, and heard her say, "I can't feel anything below my shoulders. Something snapped in my back, just below my neck." She was blinking through tears.

Normally, I would have been borderline out of control. I wasn't. Normally, I would have been shouting for the crowd to back away or for the ambulance driver to get her to the hospital immediately! I didn't. With remarkable ease, I stroked the hair away from her eyes and whispered, "I'm here with you, sweetheart. So is our Lord. No matter what happens, we'll make it through this together. I love you, Charissa." Tears ran down the side of her face as she closed her eyes.

Calmly, I stood and spoke with the emergency medical personnel. We agreed on which hospital she should go to and what route we would take. I followed in my car, again sensing the Spirit's profound and sovereign presence. Cynthia joined me at the hospital, where we waited for the x-rays and the radiologist's report. We prayed, and I told her of my encounter with the Spirit's wonderful presence.

In a few hours we learned that a vertebrae in Charissa's back had been fractured. The doctors did not know how much damage had been done to the nerves as a result of the fall and fracture. Neither did they know how long it would take for the numbness to subside or if, in fact, it would. The physicians were careful with their words, and I can still remember how grim both of them seemed. We had nothing tangible to rely on, nothing medical to count on, and nothing emotional to lean on . . . except the Spirit of God, who had stayed with us through the entire ordeal.

Sunday was just around the corner (it always is). I was exhausted by Saturday night, but again God's Spirit remained my stability. In human weakness and with enormous dependence, I preached on Sunday morning. The Lord gave me the words, and He proved His strength in my weakness. (I am told by our audio tape department that that particular message remains one of the most requested sermons on tape of all the messages I've delivered since I first became pastor of the church back in 1971.)

Amazing! God the Holy Spirit filled me, took full control, gave great grace, calmed fears, and ultimately brought wonderful healing to Charissa's back. Today she is a healthy, happy wife and mother of two, and the only time her upper back hurts is when she sneezes! When that happens and I'm with her, I usually look at her and ask, "Did that hurt?" Invariably, she nods and says, "Yeah, it did." I smile, she smiles back, and for a moment we mentally return to that original scene where she and I felt a very real awareness of the Spirit's presence.

Crisis, Peace, Prayer, Presence of God
John 14:26–27; Gal. 5:22–23; Phil. 4:6–7

Date used _____ Place _____

In his book *Enjoying God*, Lloyd Ogilvie writes:

An elder at my church realized his need for the sealing of the Spirit long after he committed his life to Christ years ago. His exemplary character and generosity made him a shoo-in for nomination and election to eldership. However, no one knew how uncertain he was about his relationship to Christ because he had kept that hidden beneath a polished exterior. He didn't anticipate that being part of the elders' prayer ministry at the end of our worship services would confront him with his own insecure relationship with Christ. When people came to pray with him, he keenly saw that something was missing in his own life. He had never allowed Christ to break through his inner hard shell of self-sufficiency. Being called to minister to others forced him to see that he was in over his head spiritually. What he was asked to pray for in others he needed himself.

Fortunately, my friend began to talk about his spiritual emptiness, although it was not easy for him to admit his neediness. He had spent his entire life convincing others that he was adequate.

As we talked, I shared with him the power of the Spirit-filled life. He'd heard hundreds of sermons about the Spirit, but the words never penetrated his shell. Now Christ was breaking the shell, allowing my elder friend to receive what Christ had longed to give him for years— the Spirit. We knelt and prayed together while he asked to receive the security and strength of being sealed. And Christ was faithful. Into the soft wax of this man's ready heart, He pressed the seal of His indwelling presence.

Emptiness, Security, Self-sufficiency
Rom. 8:13–16; Eph. 5:18

Date used _____ Place _____

Used by permission of the publisher.

Hope

We can learn something about Christian hope from fishermen. In *Pavlov's Trout,* Paul Quinnett writes:

It is better to fish hopefully than to catch fish.

Fishing is hope experienced. To be optimistic in a slow bite is to thrive on hope alone. When asked, "How can you fish all day without a hit?" the true fisherman replies, "Hold it! I think I felt something." If the line goes slack, he says, "He'll be back!"

When it comes to the human spirit, hope is all. Without hope, there is no yearning, no desire for a better tomorrow, and no belief that the next cast will bring the big strike.

According to the Bible, the Christian life is also hope experienced. A hopeless Christian is a contradiction in terms.

> Discouragement, Evangelism, Prayer
> Rom. 4:18; 15:13; 1 Cor. 13:13; Col. 1:27

Date used _____ Place _____

Strong leaders never lose hope.

The story is told of a great, never-say-die general who was taken captive and thrown into a deep, wide pit along with a number of his soldiers. In that pit was a huge pile of horse manure.

"Follow me," the general cried to his men as he dove into the pile, "There has to be a horse in here somewhere!"

Leadership, Optimism, Trials
Rom. 8:24–25; Col. 1:27; James 1:2–4

Date used _____ Place _____

In *Christianity Today*, David Neff writes:

About five years ago, Christian social critic Richard John Neuhaus was being driven from the Pittsburgh airport to a speaking engagement. During the drive, one of his hosts persisted in decrying the disintegration of the American social fabric and the disappearance of Christian values from our culture. Cases in point were too numerous to mention, but Pastor Neuhaus's host tried anyway. After the tedious drive, Neuhaus offered these words of advice: "The times may be bad, but they are the only times we are given. Remember, hope is still a Christian virtue, and despair is a mortal sin."

Cynicism, Despair, Negativism
Rom. 8:24–25; 1 Cor. 13:13; Col. 1:27

Date used _____ Place _____

Humility

In *Guideposts,* Ronald Pinkerton describes a near accident he had while hang gliding. He had launched his hang glider and been forcefully lifted 4,200 feet into the air. As he was descending, he was suddenly hit by a powerful new blast of air that sent his hang glider plummeting toward the ground.

> I was falling at an alarming rate. Trapped in an airborne riptide, I was going to crash! Then I saw him—a red-tailed hawk. He was six feet off my right wingtip, fighting the same gust I was. . . .
>
> I looked down: 300 feet from the ground and still falling. The trees below seemed like menacing pikes.
>
> I looked at the hawk again. Suddenly he banked and flew straight downwind. Downwind! If the right air is anywhere, it's upwind! The hawk was committing suicide.
>
> Two hundred feet. From nowhere the thought entered my mind: *Follow the hawk.* It went against everything I knew about flying. But now all my knowledge was useless. I was at the mercy of the wind. I followed the hawk.
>
> One hundred feet. Suddenly the hawk gained altitude. For a split second I seemed to be suspended motionless in space. Then a warm surge of air started pushing the glider upward. I was stunned. Nothing I knew as a pilot could explain this phenomenon. But it was true: I was rising.

On occasion we all have similar "downdrafts" in our lives, reversals in our fortunes, humiliating experiences. We want to lift ourselves up, but God's Word, like that red-tailed hawk, tells us to do just the opposite. God's Word tells us to dive—to humble ourselves under the hand of God. If we humble ourselves, God will send a thermal wind that will lift us up.

Ego, Instincts, Scripture, Trials
Luke 18:9–14; James 4:10

Date used _____ Place _____

Few people have the privilege of a private audience with Pope John Paul II. One who did was journalist Tim Russert, NBC News Washington bureau chief, *Meet the Press* moderator, and former altar boy. In the *St. Anthony Messenger,* James W. Arnold relates Russert's story.

> I'll never forget it. I was there to convince His Holiness it was in his interest to appear on the *Today* show. But my thoughts soon turned away from NBC's ratings toward the idea of salvation. As I stood there with the Vicar of Christ, I simply blurted, "Bless me, Father!"
>
> He put his arm around my shoulders and whispered, "You are the one called Timothy, the man from NBC?"
>
> I said, "Yes, yes, that's me."
>
> "They tell me you're a very important man."
>
> Taken aback, I said, "Your Holiness, there are only two of us in this room, and I am certainly a distant second."
>
> He looked at me and said, "Right."

It's always wise to know your place.

Blessing, Position, Status
Luke 14:7–11

Date used _____ Place _____

According to Reuters news agency, on April 28 at the 1992 Galveston County Fair and Rodeo, a steer named Husker, weighing in at 1,190 pounds, was named grand champion. The steer was sold at auction for $13,500 and slaughtered a few days after the competition. When veterinarians examined the carcass, said a contest official, they found something suspicious. They discovered evidence of what is called "airing."

To give steers a better appearance, competitors have been known to inject air into their animals' hides with a syringe or a needle attached to a bicycle pump. Pump long enough, and they've got themselves what looks like a grand champion steer, though of course it's against the rules.

The Galveston County Fair and Rodeo Association withdrew the championship title and sale money from Husker.

A pumped-up steer is like a hypocritical person. Hypocrites appear more virtuous than they are.

Boasting, Knowledge, Pride
1 Cor. 8:1

Date used _____ Place _____

Idolatry

Fans can go to the extreme in their devotion to musical performers.

In the April 25, 1994, news section of *Christianity Today,* it was reported that some fans of Elvis Presley were actually revering the king of rock and roll as a god. Pockets of semi-organized Elvis worship had taken hold in New York, Colorado, and Indiana. Worshipers raised their hands, spelled and then chanted Presley's name, worked themselves into a fervor, and prayed to the deceased star.

At the First Presleyterian Church of Denver, a Reverend Mort Farndu said that Elvis worship was spreading. Followers believe Elvis watches over them. If someone reports seeing Presley, the high priests at the Church of the Risen Elvis in Denver hold Elvis worship services. They enshrined a look-alike doll of Elvis in an altar surrounded by candles and flowers.

Idolatry is alive and well in America.

Music, Ten Commandments
Exod. 20:3; Rom. 1:18–23

Date used _____ Place _____

In the *New York Times Magazine,* Nancy V. Raine told a story she heard twenty-five years earlier from a friend named George.

> In those days, work crews marked construction sites by putting out smudge pots with open flames. George's four-year-old daughter got too close to one and her pants caught fire like the Straw Man's stuffing. The scars running the length and breadth of Sarah's legs looked like pieces of a jigsaw puzzle. In the third grade she was asked, "If you could have one wish, what would it be?" Sarah wrote: "I want everyone to have legs like mine."

When we suffer pain, we want others to understand. We want others to be like us so they can identify with us. We don't want to be alone.

God does understand. When Jesus became a man, he did something far more difficult than having legs like Sarah's.

Handicap, High Priest, Loneliness, Pain, Sympathy
John 1:14; Heb. 2:10; 4:14–5:3

Date used _____ Place _____

The March 2, 1995, issue of the *New England Journal of Medicine* reported an extraordinary case of self-treatment.

A plastic surgeon was repairing an examining-room lamp and was accidently shocked. Soon he felt dizzy, and his heart was pounding. He shakily dragged himself into his operating room and hooked himself up to a heart monitor, which showed his heart was racing at 160 beats a minute. The doctor diagnosed himself as suffering atrial fibrillation, which is potentially life threatening.

His operating room was equipped with a defibrillator, which is an electronic device that applies an electric shock to restore the rhythm of the heart. But the device was hardly designed for self-use.

Nevertheless the forty-year-old doctor quickly grabbed a tube of petroleum jelly and smeared the jelly on his bare chest. Then he grabbed the paddles of the defibrillator and pressed them to his chest. He gave himself two shocks of 100 watt-seconds (100 joules). The jolts of electricity knocked him right off the operating table, but his normal heart rhythm was restored.

Amin Karim of Baylor College of Medicine in Houston, who reported this case to the *Journal,* said this man probably would have been better off dialing 911 for an ambulance. "What if he passed out?" said Karim. "He could have put himself into a more dangerous rhythm."

Like this doctor, when we enter a crisis, we often want to rely on ourselves rather than call for help. But extreme independence is risky at best and dangerous at worst.

Church, Crisis, Faith, Prayer, Self-reliance, Works
2 Chron. 14:11; Prov. 28:26; Rom. 10:3; 2 Cor. 1:9

Date used _____ Place _____

Marsha Kaitz, a psychology professor at Hebrew University in Jerusalem, did a test to see how well mothers know their babies. According to the Associated Press, the forty-six mothers chosen for the test had all given birth in the previous five to seventy-nine hours. They all had breast-fed their newborn.

Each mother was blindfolded and then asked to identify which of three sleeping babies was her own. Nearly seventy percent of the mothers correctly chose their baby. Most of the mothers said they knew their child by the texture or temperature of the infant's hand. The women apparently learned the identifying features during routine contact, said Kaitz, because they weren't allowed to study their babies to prepare for the experiment.

The Lord knows you even better than a mother knows her baby.

Calling, Knowledge, Mothers
Ps. 131; 139; John 1:47–48

Date used _____ Place _____

At the 1994 Winter Olympics, held in Hamar, Norway, the name Dan took on very special meaning.

At his first Olympics in 1984 as an eighteen year old, Dan Jansen finished fourth in the 500 meters, beaten for a bronze medal by only sixteen one hundredths of a second, and he finished sixteenth in the 1,000.

At his second Olympics in Calgary in 1988, on the morning he was to skate the 500 meters, he received a phone call from America. His twenty-seven-year-old sister, Jane, had been fighting leukemia for over a year. She was dying. Dan spoke to her over the phone, but she was too sick to say anything in return. Their brother Mike relayed Jane's message: She wanted Dan to race for her. Before Dan skated that afternoon, however, he received the news that Jane had died. When he took to the ice, perhaps he tried too hard for his sister. In the 500 meters, he slipped and fell in the first turn. He had never fallen before in a race. Four days later in the 1,000, he fell again, this time, of all places, in the straightaway.

At his third Olympics in 1992, he was expected to win the 500 meters, where he had already set world records. For four years he had been regarded as the best sprinter in the world. But he had trouble in the final turn and he finished fourth. In the 1,000 he tied for twenty-sixth.

At his fourth Olympics in 1994, Dan again was expected to win in the 500 meters, which was his specialty. Again tragedy struck. He didn't fall, but in the beginning of the final turn he fleetingly lost control of his left skate and put his hand down, slowing him just enough to finish in eighth place. Afterward, he apologized to his home town of Milwaukee.

He had one race left, the 1,000 meter. One more race and then he would retire. At the midway point of the race, the clock showed he was skating at a world-record pace, and the crowd, including his wife and father, cheered. But with 200 meters to go, the hearts of the fans skipped a beat. Dan Jansen slipped. He didn't fall, but he slipped, touched his hand to the ice, regained control, and kept skating. When Dan crossed the finish line, he looked at the scoreboard and saw WR beside his name—world record. In his last race, Dan Jansen had finally won the gold medal.

Later that day as he stood on the award stand, Dan looked heavenward, acknowledging his late sister, Jane.

Jansen was asked to skate a victory lap. The lights were turned out, and a single spotlight illuminated Dan's last lap around the Olympic track, with a gold medal around his neck, roses in one arm, and his baby daughter—named Jane—in his other arm.

In the closing ceremony of the 1994 Olympics, Dan Jansen was chosen to carry the U.S. flag.

"Late in the afternoon of February 18, 1994," said writer Philip Hersh, "after Jansen had won the gold medal that eluded him in seven previous races over four Olympics and a decade, someone put a hand-lettered sign in the snow on the side of the main road from Lillehammer to Hamar. The sign said simply, 'Dan.' It spoke volumes about what the world thought about the man whose Olympic futility had finally ended in triumph."

Sometimes a name, a name alone, says it all. So it is when in praise we simply say, "Jesus."

Name, Perseverance, Praise
Ps. 138:2; Acts 3:16; 4:12

Date used _____ Place _____

On Tuesday, April 18, 1995, superstar Joe Montana announced his retirement from pro football after sixteen seasons. To salute him, twenty thousand residents of San Francisco filled the downtown area for a ceremony in Montana's honor.

Television announcer John Madden came to the podium and gave his opinion of Montana's skills: "This is the greatest quarterback who's ever played the game."

At one point in the ceremonies when Bill Walsh, Montana's longtime coach at the 49ers, was at the microphone, a fan yelled, "We love you, Joe."

Walsh knew that hadn't always been the case. "You weren't saying that in 1979," he replied to the fan. "Then you were saying, 'Where'd you get this guy who looks like a Swedish placekicker?'"

In 1979 Joe Montana was merely a third-round draft pick out of Notre Dame. Scouts said he had a weak arm. He was skinny. He lacked the muscular build of most football players.

But when Joe Montana stepped into the pros, he entered his element. He threw passes with perfect timing. He was the master of the two-minute drill. He went on to win four Super Bowls, helping turn the derelict 49ers into the dominant team of the 1980s.

Joe Montana was at first unimpressive to many people but was destined to be the greatest. In an infinite way, those words also describe Jesus Christ.

Appearance, Humility, Incarnation, Lordship of Christ
Isa. 53:2–3; Matt. 11:29; Phil. 2:6–11

Date used _____ Place _____

After a three-month summer recess, on October 3, 1994, the Supreme Court of the United States opened its 1994–95 term. According to the New York Times News Service, the court's legal business for that first day could be summed up with one word: *no*. The court announced it had refused to hear more than 1,600 cases. The names and docket numbers of the rejected appeals covered sixty-eight typewritten pages. For those cases, that was the last court of appeal, the final word.

There's something terribly final about judgment. The Supreme Court says no, and that's it. No appeals. No arguments. The books are sealed, and the decision is final.

On the great day of judgment there will also be a terrible crescendo of no's. "No, you cannot enter my kingdom." And the doors will be shut forever. No appeal. No time to change one's mind. Those who have rejected Jesus Christ will have forever lost their opportunity for eternal life.

Eternal life, Repentance, Salvation
Matt. 25:1–13; 2 Cor. 6:1–2; Rev. 20:11–15

Date used _____ Place _____

Judgment

To learn how Americans feel about prayer, *Life* magazine once interviewed dozens of people. One person they talked to was a prostitute, age twenty-four, in White Pine County, Nevada.

"I don't think about my feelings a lot," she said. "Instead I lie in my bed and think onto him. I meditate because sometimes my words don't come out right. But he can find me. He can find what's inside of me just by listening to my thoughts. I ask him to help me and keep me going.

"A lot of people think working girls don't have any morals, any religion. But I do. I don't steal. I don't lie. The way I look at it, I'm not sinning. He's not going to judge me. I don't think God judges anybody."

Few notions are more comforting than the idea that God judges no one. The problem is that soothing idea is false.

Morals, Prayer, Self-deception
Rom. 14:10–12

Date used _____ Place _____

In the spring of 1995 columnist Charles Krauthammer wrote an article explaining why the 1994 baseball strike dealt a fatal blow to many fans.

> The cancellation of the [World] Series reduced the entire '94 season to meaninglessness, a string of exhibition games masquerading for a while as a "championship season." No championship, no season.
>
> The real scandal of the '94 season is not the games that were canceled but the games that were played. The whole season was a phony. The fans who invested dollars and enthusiasm in the expectation that the winners and losers and homers and averages would count were cheated.
>
> More than cheated. By canceling the season in a dispute over money, the players and owners mocked the fan who really cared whether Ken Griffey broke Roger Maris's record or Tony Gwynn hit .400.

Hitting records and the World Series give meaning to the regular season. Judgment day gives meaning to life. Because God will call every deed into account, everything we do matters.

Meaning, Obedience, Significance, Ten Commandments
Eccles. 12:13–14; Rom. 14:10–12; Rev. 20:11–15

Date used _____ Place _____

The name Al Capone brings to mind crime, gangsters terrorizing a city, and Scarface himself beating three of his wayward subordinates to death with a baseball bat.

But that view of Capone wasn't always the case.

During the 1920s many people viewed Al Capone as a respected citizen, a sort of Robin Hood, says writer Ron Grossman. In 1930 students at Northwestern University's Medill School of Journalism were asked to name "the outstanding personages of the world." Capone made the list, along with George Bernard Shaw, Mahatma Gandhi, and Albert Einstein.

But Capone's days of power were shortlived.

In 1931 he attended a football game at Northwestern University. In years past when he attended sporting events, he often was saluted by fans. But this time he was booed out of the stands and left the stadium in humiliation.

In 1931, after only six years as mob boss in Chicago, Capone was convicted of income tax evasion. He ended up in Alcatraz. Eight years later when he was released from prison, he was suffering from the advanced stages of syphilis. He lived as a recluse, dying in 1947.

During his time at Alcatraz, Capone worked in the prison shoe shop and shared a cell with a convict who worked on the prison newspaper. Capone told his cellmate one evening, "I'm supposed to be a big shot and I've wound up in the shoe shop; you're supposed to be a safe cracker and now you write editorials. What kind of a screwed-up, lousy world is this?"

This world is a place where those who violate God's law may flourish for a season, but their days are numbered. Sooner or later, on this earth or at the great judgment seat, evildoers pay for their evil deeds.

Judgment, Law of God, Reaping, Sowing
Ps. 37; 73

Date used _____ Place _____

According to the Associated Press, Chuck Wall, a human relations instructor at Bakersfield College in California, was watching the news one day when a cliché from a broadcaster stuck in his mind: "Another random act of senseless violence."

Wall got an idea. He gave an unusual assignment to his students. They were to do something out of the ordinary to help someone and then write an essay about it. Then Wall dreamed up a bumper sticker that said, "Today, I will commit one random act of senseless KINDNESS . . . Will You?" The students sold the bumper stickers, which a bank and union paid to have printed, for one dollar each, and the profits went to a county Braille center.

For his random act of kindness one student paid his mother's utility bills.

Another student bought thirty blankets from the Salvation Army and took them to homeless people gathered under a bridge.

The idea took hold. The bumper sticker was slapped on all 113 county patrol cars. It was trumpeted from pulpits, in schools, and in professional associations.

After seeing the success of the idea, Chuck Wall commented, "I had no idea it would erupt like it has. I had no idea our community was in such need of something positive."

In this negative and dark world, we each can do acts of kindness to bring some light.

Golden Rule, Love, Violence
Matt. 5:14–16; 25:31–46; Gal. 5:22–23

Date used _____ Place _____

In his book *Pleasures Forevermore*, Phillip Keller writes:

For two weeks it had snowed off and on almost every day. I was beginning to weary of shoveling snow, cleaning giant cornices of snow off the roof, knocking snow off each block of wood carried in for the heater, cleaning snow from doorways and driveways. It seemed there was no end to snow, snow, snow. I even wondered where room could be found to pile the wind-driven drifts.

Then it happened. Suddenly one day I came home gingerly through the gathering gloom to find that all the driveway, the sidewalks, and even the doorways had been shoveled clean.

Stunned, I paused momentarily in the drive. It simply seemed too good to believe. The bare pavement appeared almost unreal. The huge piles of snow heaped up on every side astonished me.

Did someone, with more strength than I, care enough to come over and do this job out of sheer goodwill and heartwarming concern? Yes, someone did, and he did it with gusto.

I learned later that it was a young man from town, ten miles away. With enormous energy and strong muscles he had moved mountains of snow on my behalf. With this one gracious act of generosity he had not only saved my aching old back, but he had broken the back of winter.

In a warm and wonderful way my spirit welled up with profound gratitude. What a lift our Father gave me through that young man's strong arms!

Then another evening the doorbell rang. I went to see who was there. Cold wind tugged at the eaves and swirled around the door. I opened it carefully to keep out the formidable frost.

Standing there all wrapped up in wool cap, mitts, and thick winter jacket stood a neighbor. His bright blue eyes sparkled above crimson cheeks. "Just brought you a wee treat," he muttered, pushing a covered basket of food toward me. "I won't come in just now—too much winter." And he was gone.

Softly I unwrapped the unexpected gift. It steamed hot and pungent and tantalizing . . . a fresh, home-baked meat pie, drawn from the oven only moments before. Beside it was a piping hot bowl of rich dark gravy. What a feast! What a banquet to nourish one's body battling midwinter ice and sleet! . . .

Every mouthful of the delicious meal was relished. Every particle of pie was consumed with contentment. Every drop of gravy was licked up with glorious delight. It was a meal that will be remembered to the end of my days.

That night I curled up like a cat and slept for nine hours solid. I had peace and rest and deep, deep joy . . . besides quickened faith in the gentle goodness of generous neighbors.

In this weary old world there are still some sterling souls who really do love their neighbors as they love themselves.

Golden Rule, Love, Neighbors
Matt. 7:12; Gal. 5:22

Date used _____ Place _____

Taken from the title *Pleasures Forevermore* by Phillip Keller. Copyright © 1992 by Harvest House Publishers, Eugene, Oregon. Used by permission.

According to writer Jon Van, at the 1995 annual meeting of the American Association for the Advancement of Science, researchers revealed the results of a study that show how important kindness is in day-to-day relations.

In the experiment researchers gave forty-four doctors the symptoms of a hypothetical patient and then asked for each doctor's diagnosis of the illness. But the real point of the study was not how well the doctors could diagnose illness. Before the experiment began, researchers gave half of the doctors a bag of candy, saying it was a token of appreciation for their involvement in the study. The other doctors received nothing.

Alice Isen, a Cornell University psychologist, said the doctors receiving the candy were far more likely to correctly diagnose the patient's problem. "Pleasant-feeling states give rise to altruism, helpfulness, and improved interpersonal processes," she explained.

When God tells us to be kind to others, as always, he has a good idea. Kindness is God's program for making our world work better.

Affirmation, Encouragement, Thanks
Gal. 5:22–23; Col. 3:12

Date used _____ Place _____

The Internet is now a household word. James Coates writes that the Internet began in 1962 when Paul Baran, an engineer at the Rand Corporation think tank, found a way to move messages through a network of Defense Department computers. In 1968 the Department of Defense commissioned the Advanced Research Projects Agency to build the ARPAnet. In 1971 only twenty-three computers were on the ARPAnet.

In 1981 IBM introduced the personal computer, bringing the computer to the home. By 1984 more than one thousand computers were on the Internet.

In 1986 the ARPAnet became part of the NSFnet, which was sponsored by the National Science Foundation. This became the Internet backbone.

In 1989 more than one hundred thousand computers were on the Internet.

In 1992 more than one million computers were on the Internet. That year the Internet society was chartered to loosely govern the Internet.

In 1993 the first graphic face, called Mosaic, was put on the Internet, which made it more accessible.

In 1994 local Internet access providers and on-line services greatly expanded their Internet services.

In 1995 experts estimated that thirty million computers were on the Internet.

The kingdom of God is like the Internet. It began small with only a few disciples following Jesus. But it has spread for two thousand years, person to person, culture to culture, with more and more people getting on-line with God.

Church, Gospel, Growth
Matt. 13:31–33; Col. 1:6

Date used _____ Place _____

On December 6, 1865, just months after the Civil War ended, the thirteenth amendment outlawing slavery was ratified and became the law of the land. But that didn't mean every state approved the ratification of the amendment. Mississippi's state legislature, for example, was dominated by whites bitter over the defeat of the Confederacy, and they rejected the measure. One hundred and thirty years passed before Mississippi took action. By 1995 Mississippi was the only state in the Union that had not approved the ratification of the thirteenth amendment.

Finally, on Thursday, February 16, 1995, the Mississippi Senate voted unanimously to outlaw slavery by approving the ratification of the thirteenth amendment to the Constitution.

Senator Hillman Frazier, a member of Mississippi's Legislative Black Caucus, said, "I think it's very important for us to show the world that we have put the past behind us."

Just as there was a delay in some states ratifying an end to slavery in the United States, so there is now a delay in people accepting God's kingdom. But God's kingdom will one day hold sway over all the world, and his kingdom brings freedom.

Freedom, Liberty, Lordship of Christ
Matt. 4:17; John 3:1–7; 8:31–36; Gal. 5

Date used _____ Place _____

Nikola Tesla is the scientist who invented the method of generating electricity in what we call alternating current. Many people regard him as a greater scientific genius than the better known Alexander Graham Bell.

Author Philip Yancey tells an interesting anecdote about Tesla. During storms Tesla would sit on a black mohair couch by a window. When lightning struck, he would applaud—one genius recognizing the work of another. Tesla could appreciate better than anyone the wonder of lightning because he had spent years researching electricity.

In a similar way, the more we know God and his Word, the more deeply we will applaud his mighty deeds.

Creation, Power of God, Praise
Eph. 1:3–14

Date used _____ Place _____

In August 1994 a ship, the *Columbus Iselin,* doing environmental research ran aground off the Florida Keys and—ironically—spilled two hundred gallons of diesel fuel.

Siobhan McCready of the University of Miami said the ship was collecting "chemical, physical, and biological data on the currents of the Florida Straits." The data would be used to manage ocean oil spills.

When the *Columbus Iselin* hit a reef and punctured its two fuel tanks, it was working in the Looe Key National Marine Sanctuary—where the coral formations are famous.

Adding to the problem, efforts to pull the ship free from the reef spread a huge plume of sand, which can kill live coral.

Just as an environmental research boat can pollute the very waters it hopes to preserve, church leaders who fail morally can harm the people who follow them.

Deacons, Elders, Judgment, Moral failure, Teachers
1 Tim. 3:1–13; Titus 1:5–9; James 3:1–2

Date used _____ Place _____

Scott Turow begins his novel *Presumed Innocent* with the words of a prosecuting attorney named Rusty. Rusty is explaining his approach to the jury when he is in court. Rusty says:

> This is how I always start:
> "I am the prosecutor.
> "I represent the state. I am here to present to you the evidence of a crime. Together you will weigh the evidence. You will deliberate upon it. You will decide if it proves the defendant's guilt.
> "This man—" and here I point. . . .
> If you don't have the courage to point . . . you can't expect them to have the courage to convict.
> And so I point. I extend my hand across the courtroom. I hold one finger straight. I seek the defendant's eye. I say:
> "This man has been accused. . . ."

Scott Turow shows in the courtroom a principle that holds true in all of life. People need leaders to galvanize their courage. People need leaders to point, to take a stand, to say what they believe.

Courage, Preaching
1 Cor. 11:1; 2 Tim. 4:2

Date used _____ Place _____

In *Moody* magazine, pastor and author Leith Anderson writes:

[My wife], Charleen, and I grew up together and dated through high school and college. We've been married for most of our lives, but we've never drafted a list of rules for our lives together. Don't misunderstand, we are both committed to Jesus Christ as Lord and to the Holy Spirit as our guide. We hold God's moral law in highest value—truth, morality, honesty, honoring of parents, and preserving life.

When we first married, we could not have anticipated all that would be included in "better and worse, richer and poorer, sickness and health." There is no way that any set of rules or any book on marriage could have told us what to do. We've based our decisions on a relationship of commitment, love, and growing to know each other better every day.

That's the way the Christian life is to be lived—by relationship, not rules. The Christian's relationship with God is based on love and commitment, holding God's moral law in highest regard but depending on the grace of God to live out His morality in everyday circumstances. Every relationship is a bit different, so there is freedom. Every relationship learns and grows through experience. Life by the Spirit, not by the rules.

Holy Spirit, Rules
Gal. 5:22–25; Col. 2:6–7

Date used _____ Place _____

United Parcel Service takes pride in the productivity of its delivery men and women. On average, a UPS driver delivers four hundred packages every working day. The company gets such high productivity by micromanaging the details of a deliveryman's routine.

Writing in the *Wall Street Journal,* Robert Frank says:

"With a battalion of more than 3,000 industrial engineers, the company dictates every task for employees. Drivers must step from their trucks with their right foot, fold their money face-up, and carry packages under their left arm."

UPS "tells drivers how fast to walk (three feet per second), how many packages to pick up and deliver a day (400, on average), even how to hold their keys (teeth up, third finger)."

"Those considered slow are accompanied by supervisors, who cajole and prod them with stopwatches and clipboards."

This approach may work well in the package delivery business, but it is a complete failure in spiritual business. When spiritual leaders imitate these industrial engineers, controlling every movement of their followers, it leads to legalism and bondage. The Christian life, on the other hand, is engineered by God as a life of freedom in the Spirit.

Freedom, Obedience, Spirituality
Gal. 2:19–21; 5:1

Date used _____ Place _____

Lies

In *The Christian Reader,* Lynn Austin writes:

Sometimes Satan makes a little white lie seem like an easy way out of a problem. I know.

My five-year-old son had been looking forward to visiting the planetarium while on vacation, but when we arrived, we learned that children under age 6 were not admitted.

"Let's pretend you had a birthday," I told him. "If the ticket man asks how old you are, I want you to say, 'I'm 6.'"

I made him practice it until he sounded convincing, then bought the tickets without any problems. When the show ended, we moved on to the museum. There a large sign read, "Children 5 and under admitted free." To avoid a $5 admission fee, I had to convince my son to forget his pretend birthday.

The consequences of my lie became apparent as we walked up the steps to our last destination, the aquarium. "Wait a minute, Mom," my son said with a worried look. "How old am I now?"

I knew that I had fallen for the "way that seems right to a man, but in the end it leads to death" (Prov. 14:12).

Child rearing, Mothers
Prov. 22:6; Col. 3:9

Date used _____ Place _____

Used by permission of the author.

According to the *Chicago Tribune*, on February 21, 1995, Jeanne Calment of Arles, France, celebrated her 120th birthday. She was verifiably the oldest person in the world and had become somewhat of a celebrity in France. France's minister of health came to her birthday party. Three books had been written about her.

Medical scientists have researched her life to try to discover the secret of her longevity. They found that for years she ate two pounds of chocolate a week. She smoked moderately until age 117. She cooked with olive oil. She took vigorous walks and even rode her bike through the streets of Arles until she was 100.

At age 110 she said with good humor, "I had to wait 110 years to become famous. I intend to enjoy it as long as possible."

But by age 120 she was confined to a wheelchair. "I see badly," she said, "I hear badly, I can't feel anything, but everything's fine."

Someone asked Calment what kind of future she expected. Still displaying her good humor, she replied, "A very short one."

She speaks for us all. Even if we are young and have a hundred years to live, the body has limits, and even a long life is short.

Aging, Body, Death, Mortality
Gen. 5:27; Ps. 90:10; 144:4; 1 Cor. 15; 1 Peter 1:24–25

Date used _____ Place _____

In *Rhythms of the Heart,* Phil Hook writes:

My mother and I did not "mix." I chose a typical teenage solution to the problem—silence.

I would leave for school in the morning, come home to eat, then leave again. When I was finally home late at night, I read books.

Invariably, my mother would come downstairs and ask me if I wanted a sandwich. I grunted my assent. She cooked egg and bacon sandwiches for me night after night until I left home for good.

Years later, when our relationship was mended, she told me why she had made all those sandwiches. "If you would ever talk to me, it was while I made that sandwich," she said.

Hook writes, "I've learned love is found in a consistent display of interest, commitment, sacrifice, and attention."

Child rearing, Kindness, Mothers, Teenagers
John 13:1–17; Titus 2:4–5

Date used _____ Place _____

On the morning of Sunday, November 8, 1987, Irishman Gordon Wilson took his daughter Marie to a parade in the town of Enniskillen, Northern Ireland.

As Wilson and his twenty-year-old daughter stood beside a brick wall waiting for English soldiers and police to come marching by, a bomb planted by IRA terrorists exploded from behind, and the brick wall tumbled on them. The blast instantly killed half a dozen people and pinned Gordon and his daughter beneath several feet of bricks. Gordon's shoulder and arm were injured. Unable to move, Gordon felt someone take hold of his hand. It was his daughter Marie.

"Is that you, Dad?" she asked.

"Yes, Marie," Gordon answered.

He heard several people begin screaming.

"Are you all right?" Gordon asked his daughter.

"Yes," she said. But then she, too, began to scream. As he held her hand, again and again he asked if she was all right, and each time she said yes.

Finally Marie said, "Daddy, I love you very much."

Those were her last words. Four hours later she died in the hospital of severe spinal and brain injuries.

Later that evening a BBC reporter requested permission to interview Gordon Wilson. After Wilson described what had happened, the reporter asked, "How do you feel about the guys who planted the bomb?"

"I bear them no ill will," Wilson replied. "I bear them no grudge. Bitter talk is not going to bring Marie Wilson back to life. I shall pray tonight and every night that God will forgive them."

In the months that followed, many people asked Wilson, who later became a senator in the Republic of Ireland, how he could say such a thing, how he could forgive such a monstrous act.

Wilson explained, "I was hurt. I had just lost my daughter.

But I wasn't angry. Marie's last words to me—words of love—had put me on a plane of love. I received God's grace, through the strength of his love for me, to forgive."

For years after this tragedy, Gordon Wilson continued to work for peace in Northern Ireland.

Love can do miracles. Just as Marie Wilson's last words to her father lifted him onto the plane of love, so God's love for us lifts us onto a whole different plane, enabling us to love others no matter how they treat us.

Bitterness, Enemies, Forgiveness, Peace
Matt. 5:38–48; Rom. 12:21

Date used _____ Place _____

Bruce Thielemann tells the story of a church elder who showed what it means to follow Jesus.

A terrible ice storm had hit Pittsburgh, making travel almost impossible. At the height of the storm, a church family called their pastor about an emergency. Their little boy had leukemia and he had taken a turn for the worst. The hospital said to bring the boy in, but they could not send an ambulance, and the family did not own a car.

The pastor's car was in the shop, so he called a church elder. The elder immediately got in his car and began the treacherous journey. The brakes in his car were nearly useless. It was so slick that he could not stop for stop signs or stop lights. He had three minor accidents on the way to the family's house.

When he reached their home, the parents brought out the little boy wrapped in a blanket. His mother got in the front seat and held her son, and the father got in the back. Ever so slowly they drove to the hospital. Says Thielemann:

> They came to the bottom of a hill and as they managed to skid to a stop, he tried to decide whether he should try to make the grade on the other side, or whether he should go to the right and down the valley to the hospital. And as he was thinking about this, he chanced to look to the right and he saw the face of the little boy. The youngster's face was flushed, and his eyes wide with fever and with fear. To comfort the child, he reached over and tousled his hair. Then it was that the little boy said to him, "Mister, are you Jesus?" Do you know in that moment he could have said yes. For him to live was Jesus Christ.
>
> People who piddle around with life never know moments like that.

Loving as Jesus loved requires courage.

Courage, Risk, Sacrifice
Matt. 25:31–46; Luke 10:30–37; John 13:34–35; 15:13

Date used _____ Place _____

Love   129

In his book *The Ten Laws of Lasting Love*, Paul Pearsall describes an important episode in a battle he faced against cancer.

> Any time a doctor came with news of my progress, my wife would join with me in a mutual embrace. The reports were seldom good during the early phases of my illness, and one day a doctor brought particularly frightening news. Gazing at his clipboard, he murmured, "It doesn't look like you're going to make it."
>
> Before I could ask a question of this doomsayer, my wife stood up, handed me my robe, adjusted the tubes attached to my body and said, "Let's get out of here. This man is a risk to your health." As she helped me struggle to the door, the doctor approached us. "Stay back," demanded my wife. "Stay away from us."
>
> As we walked together down the hall, the doctor attempted to catch up with us. "Keep going," said my wife, pushing the intravenous stand. "We're going to talk to someone who really knows what is going on." Then she held up her hand to the doctor. "Don't come any closer to us."
>
> The two of us moved as one. We fled to the safety and hope of a doctor who did not confuse diagnosis with verdict. I could never have made that walk toward wellness alone.

According to the "love chapter" in the Bible, love protects.

Cancer, Faith, Hope, Marriage, Protection
Mark 5:35–43; 1 Cor. 13:7; Gal. 6:2

Date used _____ Place _____

Mother Teresa of Calcutta, India, was the keynote speaker at the 1994 National Prayer Breakfast in Washington, D.C. The scene was unforgettable: On either side of the podium sat President Clinton, Vice President Gore, and other dignitaries. Aids rolled the frail, eighty-three-year-old Mother Teresa to the podium in a wheelchair and had to help her stand to her feet. She stood on a special platform, and even with that the four-foot-six-inch woman could hardly reach the microphone.

Nevertheless her words sent shock waves through the auditorium. She rebuked America and its leaders for the policy of abortion.

"Mother Teresa said that America has become a selfish nation," writes Philip Yancey, "in danger of losing the proper meaning of love: 'giving until it hurts. . . .'"

Mother Teresa said, "If we accept that a mother can kill even her own child, how can we tell other people not to kill each other? . . . Any country that accepts abortion is not teaching its people to love but to use any violence to get what they want."

Mother Teresa pleaded with pregnant women who don't want their children: "Please don't kill the child," she said. "I want the child. Please give me the child. I want it. I will care for it."

She means what she says. Mother Teresa has already placed three thousand children with families in Calcutta.

She is a model of self-sacrificing love, speaking out on behalf of the weak and giving herself to serve them.

Abortion, Conviction, Courage, Sacrifice
John 15:13

Date used _____ Place _____

A factory employee named Kenneth worked for the largest manufacturer in Illinois for twenty-four years. The wages and benefits paid at his factory were double what the average factory job paid in America. He had steady work. He was forty-four years old, yet he had never attended a union meeting. He was a contented, middle-class worker—until 1992.

From 1992 until 1994 you could find Kenneth at the end of the day shift parading through the factory, holding an American flag along with two other workers, chanting, "No contract. No peace. No contract. No peace." Kenneth called out the cadences for about one hundred middle-age marchers.

What turned a contented worker into a thorn in this manufacturer's side? The turning point came in 1992, after the union had been on strike for nearly six months, when the company threatened to replace its striking workers.

That did something to Kenneth. It turned him bitterly against his company. Kenneth angrily explains, "I finally realized two years ago, when they threatened to replace us, that as far as they are concerned, I am nothing to them."

I am nothing to them—Kenneth's whole attitude changed when he concluded, whether rightly or wrongly, that he had no worth to the company, that he was replaceable, that they didn't care about him as a person. Even the toughest, manliest laborer in America craves loyalty, craves to have others care.

There is only one place where we are assured of that. God values us and cares for us so much that even when we "went on strike"—rejecting his will for our lives—instead of rejecting us in return, he sent his Son to die for our sins.

Bitterness, Faithfulness, Men, Significance
John 3:16; Rom. 12:10; 1 Peter 5:7

Date used _____ Place _____

In his book *Enjoying God*, Lloyd Ogilvie writes:

My formative years ingrained the quid pro quo into my attitude toward myself: *do and you'll receive; perform and you'll be loved.* When I got good grades, achieved, and was a success, I felt acceptance from my parents. My dad taught me to fish and hunt and worked hard to provide for us, but I rarely heard him say, "Lloyd, I love you." He tried to show it in actions, and sometimes I caught a twinkle of affirmation in his eyes. But I still felt empty.

When I became a Christian, I immediately became so involved in discipleship activities that I did not experience the profound healing of the grace I talked about theoretically. . . .

I'll never forget as long as I live the first time I really experienced healing grace. I was a postgraduate student at the University of Edinburgh. Because of financial pressures I had to accordion my studies into a shorter than usual period. Carrying a double load of classes was very demanding, and I was exhausted by the constant feeling of never quite measuring up. No matter how good my grades were, I thought they could be better. Sadly, I was not living the very truths I was studying. Although I could have told you that the Greek words for grace and joy are *charis* and *chara*, I was not experiencing them.

My beloved professor, Dr. James Stewart, that slightly built dynamo of a saint, saw into my soul with x-ray vision. One day in the corridor of New College he stopped me. He looked me in the eye intensely. Then he smiled warmly, took my coat lapels in his hands, drew me down to a few inches from his face, and said, "Dear boy, you are loved now!"

God loves us *now,* not when we get better. God loves us *now,* as we are.

Acceptance, Fathers, Grace, Joy
John 3:16; Rom. 5:8; 1 Peter 1:8; 1 John 4:7–10

Date used _____ Place _____

Used by permission of the publisher.

Jazz musician Billy Tipton was a gifted pianist and saxophonist who got his start during the big band era of the 1930s.

According to *Time* magazine, Billy had a few peculiarities: He refused to give his social security number to his booking agent. His three adopted sons could not recall a time when he went swimming with them. He would never visit a doctor even when suffering serious illness.

When Tipton died in 1989 at age seventy-four, the family found out why. The funeral director told one of the adopted sons that Billy Tipton was a woman. Tipton began living a lie because during the big band era, women were allowed to sing but rarely played in the band.

That kind of sexism is sad. But Billy Tipton's story is sad in another way. No matter what a person's motives are for lying, when the truth comes out, confusion, hurt, and shame are inescapable.

Ambition, Identity, Secrets, Shame, Truth
Ps. 51:6; Prov. 12:19

Date used _____ Place _____

Californians Randy Curlee and Victoria Ingram became engaged in February 1994. According to the *Chicago Tribune*, a short time later, Randy received bad news from his doctor. Randy had suffered from diabetes since he was twelve; he was now forty-six, and the doctor said the diabetes had ruined his kidneys. He would need a transplant to save his life.

Randy brought his fiancée, Victoria, to hear what the doctor was saying so she would understand how his diabetes would affect their future. The doctor said that each year only four thousand kidneys become available to the thirty-six thousand people who need a transplant. Usually family members provide the best match for a transplant, but none of Randy's family matched his profile well.

Victoria spoke up, "Why don't you test me?" The doctor gave her the tests, and the couple went home and forgot about it.

Then the phone rang. Randy's doctor reported that their immune systems were an identical match.

So the couple made plans to be married on October 11, 1994, and the next day to have the transplant surgery. At the last minute, the surgery had to be delayed because Victoria's kidney was nicked by a catheter during testing. But one month after becoming man and wife, in a five-and-a-half-hour operation at Sharp Memorial Hospital in San Diego, Victoria gave her husband, Randy, her left kidney. It was believed to be the first organ swap between husband and wife in the United States.

Randy and Victoria's marriage literally depended on her sacrifice for its survival. In a sense, so does every marriage. Marriages survive and thrive when spouses focus on what they can give to their partner more than on what they can get.

Love, Sacrifice
John 13:34–35; Eph. 5:22–33

Date used _____ Place _____

In *Focus on the Family Newsletter,* Dr. James Dobson writes:

What should a woman do for a man that will relate directly to his masculine nature? In a word, she can build his confidence. This vital role is best illustrated by one of my favorite stories told by my friend E. V. Hill. Dr. Hill is a dynamic black minister and the senior pastor at Mt. Zion Missionary Baptist Church in Los Angeles. He lost his precious wife, Jane, to cancer a few years ago. In one of the most moving messages I've ever heard, Dr. Hill spoke about Jane at her funeral and described the ways this "classy lady" made him a better man.

As a struggling young preacher, E. V. had trouble earning a living. That led him to invest the family's scarce resources, over Jane's objections, in the purchase of a service station. She felt her husband lacked the time and expertise to oversee his investment, which proved to be accurate. Eventually, the station went broke, and E. V. lost his shirt in the deal.

It was a critical time in the life of this young man. He had failed at something important, and his wife would have been justified in saying, "I told you so." But Jane had an intuitive understanding of her husband's vulnerability. Thus, when E. V. called to tell her that he had lost the station, she said simply, "All right."

E. V. came home that night expecting his wife to be pouting over his foolish investment. Instead, she sat down with him and said, "I've been doing some figuring. I figure that you don't smoke and you don't drink. If you smoked and drank, you would have lost as much as you lost in the service station. So, it's six in one hand and a half-dozen in the other. Let's forget it."

Jane could have shattered her husband's confidence at that delicate juncture. The male ego is surprisingly fragile, especially during times of failure and embarrassment. That's why E. V. needed to hear her say, "I still believe in you," and that is precisely the message she conveyed to him.

Shortly after the fiasco with the service station, E. V. came home one night and found the house dark. When he opened the door, he saw that Jane had prepared a candlelight dinner for two.

"What meaneth thou this?" he said with characteristic humor.

"Well," said Jane, "we're going to eat by candlelight tonight."

E. V. thought that was a great idea and went into the bathroom to wash his hands. He tried unsuccessfully to turn on the light. Then he felt his way into the bedroom and flipped another switch. Darkness prevailed. The young pastor went back to the dining room and asked Jane why the electricity was off. She began to cry.

"You work so hard, and we're trying," said Jane, "but it's pretty rough. I didn't have quite enough money to pay the light bill. I didn't want you to know about it, so I thought we would just eat by candlelight."

Dr. Hill described his wife's words with intense emotion: "She could have said, 'I've never been in this situation before. I was reared in the home of Dr. Caruthers, and we never had our light cut off.' She could have broken my spirit; she could have ruined me; she could have demoralized me. But instead she said, 'Somehow or another we'll get these lights on. But let's eat tonight by candlelight.'"

Courage, Forgiveness, Wives
1 Cor. 13:4–7; Eph. 5:22–33

Date used _____ Place _____

The story is told of a prosperous, young investment banker who was driving a new BMW sedan on a mountain road during a snow storm. As he veered around one sharp turn, he lost control and began sliding off the road toward a deep precipice. At the last moment he unbuckled his seat belt, flung open his door, and leaped from the car, which then tumbled down the ravine and burst into a ball of flames.

Though he had escaped with his life, the man suffered a ghastly injury. Somehow his arm had been caught near the hinge of the door as he jumped and had been torn off at the shoulder.

A trucker saw the accident in his rearview mirror. He pulled his rig to a halt and ran to see if he could help. He found the banker standing at the roadside, looking down at the BMW burning in the ravine below.

"My BMW! My new BMW!!" the banker moaned, oblivious to his injury.

The trucker pointed at the banker's shoulder and said, "You've got bigger problems than that car. We've got to find your arm. Maybe the surgeons can sew it back on!"

The banker looked where his arm had been, paused a moment, and groaned, "Oh no! My Rolex! My new Rolex!!"

God gives us material possessions so we will enjoy them, not so we will worship them.

Greed, Priorities, Values
Luke 12:13–21

Date used _____ Place _____

Men are strong in different ways.

Sports Illustrated once did a profile on a champion arm wrestler named Dave Patton. According to the article Patton hadn't lost an arm-wrestling match in some twelve years. He weighed a mere 160 pounds but easily defeated men twice his size.

Patton trained obsessively. He did exactly 756 bicep curls per session, pushing his pain threshold to the outer limits. For fun he ventured onto the streets of Manhattan, set up a table, and challenged all comers to a prize of one thousand dollars to whoever could beat him. No one of any size ever had.

In the article Tom Junod describes the feats of strength of other men.

> Moe Baker of Bristol, Connecticut, . . . not only had 18-inch forearms but could also jump straight out of a 55-gallon drum without ever touching the sides. Cleve Dean, a 600-pound hog farmer from Georgia, was a he-man, too, because he could pick up a full-grown sow under each arm and walk around. . . . And the legendary Mac Batchlor, from Los Angeles, was a he-man because he could fold four bottle caps in half simply by placing them on his fingers and closing his fist.

These are strong men. God wants men to be strong—but strong in a way that matters.

Power, Strength
1 Cor. 16:13; Eph. 6:10

Date used _____ Place _____

At the Wright Patterson Air Force base in Dayton, Ohio, researchers hope they will develop the means for pilots to fly airplanes with their minds. The project is called brain-actuated control.

Writers Ron Kotulak and Jon Van say this is how it could work. The pilot would wear scalp monitors that pick up electrical signals from various points on his head. The scalp monitors would be wired to a computer. Using biofeedback techniques, the pilot would learn to manipulate the electrical activity created by his or her thought processes. The computer would translate the electrical signals into mechanical commands for the airplane.

Imagine being able to bank an airplane's wings, accelerate, and climb another ten thousand feet, all by controlling what you think.

Although controlling airplanes with the mind is yet to be developed, our mind already has tremendous control of one thing: our behavior. Our thoughts sooner or later lead to our actions.

Heart, Self-control, Thoughts
Prov. 4:23; Rom. 13:14; James 1:14–15

Date used _____ Place _____

According to an October 29, 1994, story from the Reuters news agency, a Chinese woman named Zhang Meihua began to suffer mysterious symptoms when she turned twenty. She was losing the ability to nimbly move her legs and arms. Doctors could not find the cause, and the symptoms continued.

Two decades passed, and Zhang began to also suffer from chronic headaches. Again she sought help from the doctors. This time a CAT scan and an X ray found the source of the woman's mysterious symptoms. A rusty pin was lodged in her head. The head of the pin was outside the skull, and the shaft penetrated into her brain. Doctors performed surgery and successfully extracted the pin.

The Xinhua news agency reported the doctors expressed amazement that the woman "could live for so long a time with a rusty pin stuck in her brain." After noting the position of the pin in her skull, they speculated that the pin had entered her skull sometime soon after birth and before her skull had hardened. Zhang, now fully recovered, said she "had no memory of being pierced by a pin in the head."

Like the rusty pin in that woman's brain, unwholesome thoughts, bad attitudes, and painful memories can lodge in our minds and cause chronic problems. God tells us to renew our minds.

Attitudes, Health, Thoughts
Rom. 12:1–2; Phil. 4:8–9

Date used _____ Place _____

In a *Forbes* article about Harry Quadracci and the Quad/ Graphics printing company, Phyllis Berman writes about the kind of employees the company hires.

> A good many people whom society would dismiss as losers have been given a chance at Quad/Graphics, and they are grateful.
>
> "We hire people who have no education and little direction," Quadracci explains. "They are the kind of people who look at their shoes when they apply for a job. They join the firm not for its high wages— starting salaries on the floor are only about $7.50 an hour—but because we offer them a chance to make something out of themselves."

Like this businessman, God delights in calling workers who look at their shoes when they apply for the job. God gives great responsibility to people whom the world thinks little of.

Calling, Confidence, Losers, Pride, Salvation, Spiritual gifts
Exod. 3; 1 Cor. 1:18–31; 2 Cor. 3:5–6

Date used _____ Place _____

We can learn something about effective ministry from a famous trumpet player for the Chicago symphony.

Adolph (Bud) Herseth is regarded as "the premier orchestral trumpeter of his time, and perhaps of all time," wrote Jim Doherty in 1994. Herseth has played first trumpet for the world-class Chicago Symphony for nearly fifty years.

"Fellow musicians hail him as 'a legend,' 'a phenomenon' and the 'prototype,'" says the writer. "Critics knock themselves out singing his praise. He is a hero to brass students at music schools. Wherever the Chicago goes on tour, young players mob him."

Doherty continues:

> Early in his career, a car accident cost him a half-dozen front teeth and split his lower lip so badly thirteen stitches were needed to close it. A mere mortal might have feared the end of his playing days. Bud had his mouth rebuilt and six weeks later resumed his seat. His lip was numb and his mouthpiece felt funny, yet somehow he produced the same gorgeous sound. He can't explain it.
>
> That pretty much sums up Bud's whole approach. He refuses to make a big deal about "technique." Playing has less to do with the mouth than the ear, he says. "You have to start with a very precise sense of how something should sound. Then, instinctively, you modify your lip and your breathing and the pressure of the horn to obtain that sound."

Techniques and rules are not the key to playing the trumpet, nor are they the key to serving Christ. First and foremost, you've got to hear it. You've got to know what the "music" of ministry sounds like. Techniques are secondary.

Discipleship, Holy Spirit, Legalism, Spiritual discernment,
Technique, Training, Vision
Mark 3:13–15

Date used _____ Place _____

The highest honor a French chef can attain is to have his restaurant listed as a three-star restaurant in the Michelin Guide to fine eating. According to the *Chicago Tribune*, the 1995 Guide added a twentieth restaurant to its three-star listing: the Auberge de l'Eridan in Annecy, France.

The owner and self-taught chef, Marc Veyrat, is a culinary maverick. His unorthodox ideas got him kicked out of three hotel culinary schools, and local hotels would not even take him on as an apprentice in the kitchen.

Veyrat is from the French Alps. Alpine herbs, such as caraway, cumin, wild thyme, and chenopodium, are key ingredients in his recipes. Once a week at dawn Veyrat ventures into the mountains to pick the herbs.

"I know I'm not a traditional chef," says Veyrat. "I'm a student of nature, because before you love cuisine, you have to love the ingredients."

The teaching of God's Word is much like preparing fine food. Before you can bring people the gospel, you first must love the Word.

Creativity, Love, Preaching, Study, Teaching
Rom. 1:9; 1 Tim. 4:15–16; 2 Tim. 3:14; 4:2

Date used _____ Place _____

In the spring of 1995 congressional Democrats and Republicans were battling over the national budget. According to Reuters, one portion of a tax-cut bill stirred up a storm of controversy. The debated provision was designed to crack down on wealthy Americans who renounce U.S. citizenship to avoid taxes. That's right. Some American billionaires actually move their citizenship to another country to save money. One politician referred to them as "Benedict Arnold billionaires."

Money can do terrible things to a person's loyalties.

Greed, Idolatry, Loyalty
Matt. 6:19–24; 1 Tim. 6:6–10

Date used _____ Place _____

Money can't buy happiness. You've probably heard that cliché in the mouths of the old and the wise, but now even social scientists are saying that money doesn't make you happy.

According to writers Ron Kotulak and Jon Van, an international study based on information gathered in thirty-nine countries and published in the journal *Social Indicators Research* concluded that the more money people make, the more they want, so happiness keeps eluding them.

The study said, "Neither increasing income at the individual level nor country level were accompanied by increases in subjective well-being."

In fact the researchers found that rapid increases in wealth resulted in less, not more, happiness.

Ed Diener, a University of Illinois psychologist, said, "A lot of people think, *If only I had a million dollars, I'd be happy.* It could be true for an individual, but for most people, on average, it appears not to be true."

Coveting, Greed, Happiness
Luke 16:13–15; Heb. 13:5–6

Date used _____ Place _____

When we feel desperate, we sometimes do dangerous things.

In the fall of 1993 Armenia was a country desperate for power sources. The country was entering its third winter under a near-total oil and gas blockade imposed by neighboring Azerbaijan as a weapon in the war between the two former Soviet republics. To survive, the people of Armenia had been cutting down trees for fuel to heat their homes—over 1.5 million trees were lost during the previous winter. As a result, the government was considering the unthinkable: starting up a rusting Soviet nuclear reactor shut down in 1989 because it was unsafe.

The Medzamor nuclear plant was built in the 1970s. The out-dated plant had no containment building to control the effects of an accidental radiation leak. The plant was in a known earth-quake zone located a mere twenty-five miles from Armenia's capital city, Yerevan, and so any accident would expose hundreds of thousands of people to deadly radiation.

In desperation, people often choose things they live to regret. Turning to sin in a time of need is like pinning your hopes on a rusty, outdated, nuclear power plant.

Addictions, Chemical dependency, Depression,
Desperation, Prayer, Sin, Trouble
Num. 13–14; Ps. 107; Mark 4:17; James 5:13

Date used _____ Place _____

In *General Patton's Principles for Life and Leadership,* Gen. George S. Patton Jr. says:

> Picking the right leader is the most important task of any commander. I line up the candidates and say, "Men, I want a trench dug behind warehouse ten. Make this trench eight feet long, three feet wide and six inches deep."
>
> While the candidates are checking their tools out at the warehouse, I watch them from a distance. They puzzle over why I want such a shallow trench. They argue over whether six inches is deep enough for a gun emplacement. Some complain that such a trench should be dug with power equipment. Others gripe that it is too hot or too cold to dig. If the men are above the rank of lieutenant, there will be complaints that they should not be doing such lowly labor. Finally, one man will order, "What difference does it make what [he] wants to do with this trench! Let's get it dug and get out of here."
>
> That man will get the promotion. Pick the man who can get the job done!

God too is looking for people to whom he can give authority and responsibility. Like Patton, he gives people jobs and watches to see how they respond. Most of all, God is looking for obedience and faithfulness.

Complaining, Faithfulness, Leadership
Matt. 26:17–19; 1 Cor. 16:15–16; 1 Tim. 3:10

Date used _____ Place _____

On Sunday night, March 22, 1992, a twin-engine jetliner, USAir flight 405, waited in line to take off from New York's LaGuardia Airport. On board was Bart Simon, a Cleveland businessman. Outside, a snowstorm was blowing. After the plane sat in line for nearly thirty minutes, the control tower gave clearance for takeoff.

The Dutch-made Fokker F28 raced its engines and headed southeast down runway 13-31. The plane lifted into the air, but then the left wing dipped and scraped against the runway. The landing gear struck a set of navigational lights, and the plane touched back down to the left of the runway, splattering along in the mud for one hundred feet.

The plane then nosed briefly back up into the air, but the left wing hit antennas on the side of the runway, and the fuselage began to break apart. Finally the plane bounced into Flushing Bay.

Twenty-seven people were killed in the crash. But Bart Simon survived unharmed.

Surviving a plane crash is a traumatic experience. No one would blame Bart Simon if he chose never to fly again. No one would think twice if he decided the next day to drive home to Cleveland or to take a bus or train.

But on Monday, the day after the crash, Bart Simon climbed aboard another airplane and flew—safely—home to Cleveland.

Bart Simon is an overcomer.

Fear grounds many people. Fear paralyzes ministries, relationships, dreams, churches, careers. The only way to overcome is to do what we fear.

Fear, Perseverance, Tragedy
Phil. 1:6, 20; 1 Peter 3:14; Rev. 2:7; 12:11

Date used _____ Place _____

Elizabeth Mittelstaedt is the editor of *Lydia*, the largest Christian magazine in Europe, published in three languages—German, Romanian, and Hungarian. She and her husband, Ditmar, live near Frankfurt, Germany. In *Today's Christian Woman*, Elizabeth writes:

Ten years ago, I spent five hours in a dentist's chair for what was supposed to be a routine dental procedure and was left with a severely damaged nerve in my jaw. As a result, shooting pain— worse than a severe toothache—pulsated constantly on the right side of my face.

To rid myself of the excruciating pain, I traveled from one doctor to another for six months—to no avail. Nobody was able to prescribe something to ease my torment and despair.

Finally, a doctor at the Mayo Clinic in Minnesota told me, "Mrs. Mittelstaedt, there's nothing more that can be done to repair the damage or relieve your pain. You'll have to live with it."

When I returned home to Germany with this news, I felt discouraged and deeply depressed. Medical records show that many people who suffer with the same problem resort to suicide. I, too, felt death was the only escape, but as a Christian, I couldn't believe that was God's will for me.

But the constant pain took its toll. I felt hopeless, with nothing left to hang on to. One day, during my morning walk, I crossed a small bridge near Frankfurt, looked down at the flowing river below, and heard a voice say to me, "Why don't you just jump?" But when I looked down at the water, I realized it was too shallow to drown in. Then the voice said, "Don't worry. It's stony down there. You'll hit your head and die anyway."

At that moment, Matthew 4:5–7 came to my mind. I recalled how the devil had unsuccessfully tempted Jesus to jump from the highest point of the temple. So I said, "No, I am not going to jump. I am going to trust God."

I began telling God what I was most afraid of—living in pain. Then I remembered that Jesus says we shouldn't worry about tomorrow—that he gives us strength for one day. I thought, *Somehow, I'll make it through the day.*

As I looked out over our town and saw the beautiful steepled fairy-tale homes with flower-filled window boxes, white picket fences, and clean-swept sidewalks, I realized that behind this perfect facade were thousands of Europeans struggling with the aftermath of two World Wars—broken marriages, depression, guilt, loneliness, and crushed hopes. I felt the Lord tell me, "Elizabeth, these women are suffering like you are today, and they want to give up. But their pain is different—it's emotional."

I no longer felt so alone in my pain. And suddenly I was filled with a desire to encourage those women. That morning, the vision for a Christian woman's magazine in Europe was born.

Almost a decade has passed since that day by the bridge. Today, *Lydia* is printed in three languages and reaches about one million readers. Its message is simple—hope and encouragement can be found through faith in Christ and his Word. When I receive letters from readers who say, "I didn't abort my baby, and I'm naming her Lydia after the magazine," or "Thank you—this magazine is my only friend," my heart is thrilled. It's been so healing for me.

Pain is still my companion—but it's no longer as overwhelming as it once was. When I searched God's Word for encouragement and comfort, I came upon Psalm 34:19: "Many are the afflictions of the righteous, but the Lord delivers him out of them all" (KJV). The words to the left of the comma describe my circumstances—and the words to the right give me real hope for the future. But I've learned that when we hang on to the comma in the middle—wait in faith on God's promise and offer our pain to him—it's never wasted.

Fear, Health, Perseverance, Suffering, Suicide
Ps. 34:19

Date used _____ Place _____

This article first appeared in *Today's Christian Woman* magazine (Jan. / Feb. 1995), published by Christianity Today, Inc., Carol Stream, Ill.

Alan Mairson wrote an article for *National Geographic* about beekeepers who raise and transport bees for a living. He told the story of Jeff and Christine Anderson and how their daughter overcame an allergy to bee stings.

To build up her immunity, doctors administered a series of injections to Rachel over a four-month period. But, in order to maintain immunity, she needed a shot or a bee sting every six weeks over several years.

So every six weeks Rachel's parents would go outside and catch a bee. Then, as Rachel recalls, "Mom would take hold of my arm and roll my sleeve up. Then my Dad would make the bee mad and stick it on me and count to ten before he took the stinger out. But it worked. Now when I accidentally get stung, it barely swells, it barely hurts."

In a world full of bees, a loving father must not shield his child from every sting. In fact for the child's own good the father must at times induce pain.

God the Father, Love of God, Temptation, Trials
Rom. 8:28; James 1:2–4; 1 Peter 1:5–9

Date used _____ Place _____

In his book *Broken in the Right Place*, Alan Nelson writes:

Somehow, pain, problems, and suffering do not fit into our concept of life and success.

My sons, with the help of their mom, have designated places for their belongings. Toys go in specific plastic tubs, clothes in the dresser and closet, and books in the book box. Even when the room is a mess, someone can quickly order it, primarily because everything has its place. But what do you do with an item which does not have an assigned spot? You stand in the middle of the room, holding it, perplexed, unsure of what to do with this foreign body. That is how most people handle their pain, discouragements and disillusionment. Their sense of direction halts. They stall as they search in vain for a place to put it, to make it fit into their orderly lives. . . .

Why in the world do bad things happen to good people? We can understand why they happen to bad people. . . . But somewhere we learn that good things should happen to good people, and of course, we're on the good people list. That's why we often do not deal well with obstacles and turmoil; we have no place to put them in our "good person" scheme of things.

Goodness, Suffering
2 Cor. 1:3–11; Phil. 1:29; Heb. 12:1–11

Date used _____ Place _____

Used by permission of the publisher.

A recent Roper poll showed that parents may not be doing all they can to encourage their teens to remain sexually pure. Seventy-two percent of the teens who reported having sexual intercourse said they did it in the homes of their parents or their partner's parents. Six out of ten believe their parents know about their sexual behavior.

When parents say nothing about wrongdoing, in effect they condone wrongdoing.

Sex, Teenagers, Virginity
1 Thess. 4:3–8

Date used _____ Place _____

Michael Jordan's father, James Jordan, was murdered in the summer of 1993. Before that happened, Michael said this to columnist Bob Greene:

> My heroes are and were my parents. . . . It wasn't that the rest of the world would necessarily think that they were heroic. But they were the adults I saw constantly, and I admired what I saw.
>
> If you're lucky, you grow up in a house where you can learn what kind of person you should be from your parents. And on that count, I was very lucky. It may have been the luckiest thing that ever happened to me.

To Michael Jordan, good parents meant as much to him as his incomparable basketball skill.

Child rearing, Example, Heroes
Eph. 6:4

Date used _____ Place _____

A common sight in America's Southwest desert is the century plant. It's unique. The century plant (*Agave Americana*) thrives in rocky, mountainous, desert sites. It has dramatic, splayed leaves that grow up to a foot wide. The plant can reach twelve feet in diameter.

But what makes the century plant unusual, as its name suggests, is its long reproduction cycle. For twenty or thirty years (no, not a literal one hundred years), the six-foot-tall plant stands the same height and puts out no flowers. Then one year, without warning, a new bud sprouts. The bud, which resembles a tree-trunk-size asparagus spear, shoots into the sky at a fantastic rate of seven inches per day and reaches an eventual height of twenty to forty feet. Then it crowns itself with several clumps of yellowish blossoms that last up to three weeks.

Like the century plant, many of the most glorious things that happen to us come only after a long wait.

Aging, Fruitfulness, Growth, Maturity
Gen. 21:1–7; Gal. 5:22–23; 6:9–10; Heb. 10:36

Date used _____ Place _____

In 1994 the British Broadcasting Corporation produced a radio program perfectly designed for the patience level of people in our fast-changing, fast-paced culture. The drama series, entitled "The Telephone Box," had three episodes. Each episode was one minute long. The entire story lasted three minutes.

Script writer Wally Daly said, "It is a real play and fulfills all the criteria, having a beginning, middle, and end."

All three episodes played on the same day, interspersed with music, because if there were a week between episodes, Daly explained, listeners would not remember what had happened.

Sometimes we want God to work in our lives at the same speed as "The Telephone Box." But God often works on a far different timetable.

Growth, Perseverance, Prayer, Sovereignty of God, Suffering, Time
Gal. 5:22–23; James 5:7–8

Date used _____ Place _____

In 1995 Steve Kafka was voted into the Illinois High School gymnastics coaches Hall of Fame. Kafka coached the Glenbard East High School gymnastics team in Glen Ellyn to second-place finishes in 1987, 1988, and 1990. Then in 1995, after rebuilding a team at a different school, he took second one more time and finally in 1996 won the state championship.

To accomplish that, his gymnasts had to hit their routines in the state championship competition, when pressure is high and it's easy to fall. Actually the first time Kafka's team qualified for state, several Glenbard East gymnasts fell off the side horse, high bar, and parallel bars, and the team finished down in the standings.

But then coach Kafka got an idea. At the end of practice each day, he began conducting a practice meet, and he did two things to intentionally raise the pressure on the gymnasts. First, if anyone missed a routine, everyone had to do push-ups. Second, Kafka told the team to try and rattle each performer. And so while one gymnast performed on the side horse, his teammates would yell, threaten bodily harm, tell jokes, even throw rolled up socks at him.

"My gymnasts started to feel that competing in real meets was a breeze compared to practice," says Kafka. In the end, even a state championship—with TV cameras rolling and critical judges watching every move—was easy. Fighting through daily opposition taught Kafka's gymnasts focus and determination.

In the same way, persecution can lead true followers of Christ to a greater focus on Christ and a stronger determination to do his will without fail.

Character, Determination, Focus, Hardships
John 15:20; Heb. 12:1–13

Date used _____ Place _____

Victor Villasenor is a Hispanic writer who is a story in himself.

Raised in Southern California, says writer Jorge Casuso, Victor Villasenor was illiterate because of dyslexia until adulthood. Then a woman in Mexico taught him to read. Ironically, he decided he wanted to become a great writer and he asked God to help him.

While he worked for ten years as a laborer, digging ditches and cleaning houses, his mind was free to think and dream up characters and plots. At home he read voraciously, devouring more than five thousand books. He memorized favorite openings and analyzed paragraphs and sentences, taking them apart to see how they worked. And most important, he started writing. He wrote nine novels, sixty-five short stories, and ten plays. He sent them all to publishers. All were rejected. One publisher sent him a rejection letter that simply said, "You're kidding."

Incredibly he was encouraged by that. It meant that at least the publisher had read his submission. Then in 1972 after 260 rejections, Villasenor sold his first novel, which was called *Macho*. He then published a nonfiction work called *Jury: People vs. Juan Corona,* an award-winning screenplay called *Ballad of Gregorio Cortez*, and, the crowning work of his life, a two-part saga of his family called *Rain of Gold* that took twelve years to write.

With a lot of hard work on Villasenor's part, God answered his prayer.

Diligence, Failure, Overcomers, Work
Heb. 10:36

Date used _____ Place _____

Even the most talented people may not get it right the first time.

In a 1995 interview ex-Beatle Paul McCartney said he once wrote a song with the first line "Scrambled eggs, oh my baby how I love your legs."

Have you ever heard that song?

Not likely. McCartney tossed those words and wrote, "Yesterday, all my troubles seemed so far away."

Since then "Yesterday" has played on the radio more than six million times, more than any other record in history. "Yesterday" also happens to be McCartney's favorite song.

The difference between failure and success—between "Scrambled Eggs" and "Yesterday"—is persistence.

Ministry, Perseverance, Success, Writing
Acts 13:13; 1 Cor. 15:58; Gal. 6:9–10; Heb. 10:36

Date used _____ Place _____

In 1984, 1988, and 1992 American speed skater Dan Jansen suffered a series of disappointments in his attempts to win Olympic gold. How did he keep coming back time and time again? He says he learned to keep things in perspective. In *Full Circle,* Jansen writes:

> When I was nine years old, I was competing at the youth national championships in Minnesota. I was in good position to win my first national title when, coming around a turn, I tripped on a rubber hose they had set up as a lane marker. That slip cost me the title by one point.
>
> I started crying. I was crying as Mom took off my skates and during the award ceremonies. I was still crying when we got in the car and when we pulled into our driveway six hours later.
>
> My father hadn't spoken a word to me all the way home. But as we got out of the car, he said quietly, "You know, Dan, there's more to life than skating around in a circle."

As bitter as any loss may be, when we know the Lord there is always much more to life than any disappointment we are now facing.

Disappointments, Loss, Priorities, Sports
Rom. 8:18; Phil. 3:7–11

Date used _____ Place _____

On October 28, 1993, the U.S. Space Command watched as a two-ton chunk of Chinese satellite began to reenter the earth's atmosphere. The Space Command tracks more than seven thousand man-made objects orbiting near Earth, and according to their calculations this satellite would drop into the Pacific Ocean five hundred miles west of Baja California. When it plunged into the atmosphere, however, it skipped south and took an unexpected detour, landing in the Pacific Ocean west of Peru.

Major Bob Butt explained that space debris traveling seventeen thousand miles per hour takes unpredictable twists and turns when it breaks into the thickening atmosphere. It's like dropping a penny into water. "Sometimes it goes straight down, and sometimes it turns end over end and changes direction."

This wasn't the first time the Chinese satellite had thwarted the predictions of scientists. It was launched October 8, 1993, carrying into space microgravity experiments. Ten days after launch, a capsule containing the experiments was to have separated and parachuted to earth for retrieval. But on October 18 when Chinese scientists radioed the reentry commands, the satellite went out of control, split in two, and stayed in orbit. The Chinese space agency predicted it would remain in orbit six more months. In fact it stayed in orbit only ten more days, coming down a few hours earlier than even the U.S. Space Agency thought.

Our lives are a lot like that Chinese satellite: unpredictable, defying our best laid plans, filled with surprises. That's why God tells us to approach our planning and praying with great humility.

God's will, Humility, Prayer, Submission, Surprise
Prov. 16:9; 19:21; James 4:13–17

Date used _____ Place _____

According to *U.S. News and World Report,* medical studies have suggested that all cholesterol is not the same. There is "good cholesterol" and "bad cholesterol."

Good cholesterol consists of high-density lipoproteins, or HDLs. Bad cholesterol consists of low-density lipoproteins, or LDLs.

Bad cholesterol clogs arteries and leads to heart attacks.

"Good cholesterol," writes Rita Rubin, "seems to carry cholesterol out of the coronary-artery walls, thus preventing blockages. Studies show the rate of coronary heart disease falls as HDL levels rise."

Just as all cholesterol is not the same, the Bible says all pleasure is not the same. There is good pleasure and bad pleasure. Good pleasure is healthful, self-controlled, and obedient to God's commands. Bad pleasure is self-indulgent, addictive, and disobedient to God's commands.

Asceticism, Thanksgiving
Ps. 16:11; 103:5; 1 Tim. 4:3–5; 2 Tim. 3:4; Titus 3:3

Date used _____ Place _____

People will go to amazing lengths to get "high." In 1994, says writer Gene Sloan in *USA Today*, undercover agents for the Arizona Department of Fish and Game arrested several people for toad licking—that's right, toad licking.

They had in their possession the Colorado River toad (*Bufo alvarius*). This toad, which is found from the Mexican border to the Grand Canyon, deters predators by secreting a milky white substance that includes a powerful drug classified as psychoactive under Arizona law. Drug aficionados get high by either licking the toads directly or drying the secretion and then smoking it.

One Arizona official warned that the drug is "poisonous and dangerous."

An addiction to pleasure is a sinful condition that can lead a person to do any number of vile—even deadly—things.

Addictions, Chemical dependency, Prostitution
2 Tim. 3:4; Titus 3:3; 2 Peter 2:13

Date used _____ Place _____

On April 1, 1988, Dr. Gary Hamlin, an osteopath in Joplin, Missouri, opened a new medical practice where any patient who needed medical care received it. No one was turned over to a collection agency for non-payment. Medicare and Medicaid assignments were welcomed. Thirty-five to forty-five patients came to his clinic each day. To pay his overhead, Dr. Hamlin had to moonlight every other weekend in a local hospital.

In *The Christian Reader*, Dr. Hamlin explained what caused him to open such a practice.

"Luke 14:14 introduced me to the founding principle for the clinic. It was God's personal promise to me. 'And thou shalt be blessed; for they cannot recompense thee: for thou shalt be recompensed at the resurrection of the just.'"

Blessing, Giving
Luke 14:12–14

Date used _____ Place _____

In *Christianity Today,* Philip Yancey writes about a time when the church he attended in Chicago faced something of a crisis.

The pastor had left, attendance was flagging, a community outreach program now seemed threatened. The leadership suggested an all-night vigil of prayer.

Several people raised questions. Was it safe, given our inner-city neighborhood? Should we hire guards or escorts for the parking lot? What if no one showed up? At length we discussed the logistics and the "practicality" of such an event. Nevertheless, the night of prayer was scheduled.

To my surprise, the poorest members of the congregation, a group of senior citizens from a housing project, were the ones who responded most enthusiastically to the prayer vigil. I could not help wondering how many of their prayers had gone unanswered over the years—they lived in the projects, after all, amid crime, poverty, and suffering—yet they showed a childlike trust in the power of prayer. "How long do you want to stay—an hour or two?" we asked. "Oh, we'll stay all night," they replied.

One black woman in her nineties, who walks with a cane and can barely see, explained . . . "You see, they's lots of things we can't do in this church. We ain't so educated, and we ain't got as much energy as some of you younger folks. But we can pray. We got time, and we got faith. Some of us don't sleep much anyway. We can pray all night if needs be."

And so they did. Meanwhile, a bunch of yuppies in a downtown church learned anew a lesson of faith from the Gospels: Faith appears where least expected and falters where it should be thriving.

Faith, Prayer
Luke 6:20–26; 10:21; James 2:5

Date used _____ Place _____

Who wouldn't like to own a Jaguar XJS convertible? In many people's eyes, a snazzy Jaguar is something they dream for a lifetime about getting and for which they are willing to pay the steep price tag of fifty-six thousand dollars.

Marvin Jacobs, a San Francisco lawyer, bought his dream Jaguar, only to find that it didn't exactly make his life complete. *USA Today* reported in an article on state "lemon laws" that over the next three-and-a-half years Jacobs had to take his car to the shop a grand total of twenty-six times. Once the car even stalled on the Golden Gate Bridge during rush hour, causing a five-mile backup. When California's lemon law finally forced Jaguar to buy back the sour car, Jacobs said unloading it was "the best thing that ever happened to me in my entire adult life."

Material possessions—the things we so often dream of buying—can carry a much higher price tag than we anticipate.

Coveting, Materialism
Luke 12:15

Date used _____ Place _____

On Wednesday, October 11, 1994, NASA's *Magellan* space explorer fell silent. The *Magellan* had circled Venus more than fifteen thousand times since arriving at the planet in 1990, but on this day NASA scientists intentionally changed the satellite's course and sent it veering into the planet where it burned to a crisp in the atmosphere.

Why would NASA send the *Magellan*—which cost nine hundred million dollars—plummeting into the planet? Because the *Magellan* was virtually out of power. One final experiment had drained its batteries to the point where it could no longer transmit data.

Without power, even the highest technology is worthless. Without the power of God, even the most committed Christian can bear no fruit.

Death, Endurance, Fruitfulness, Holy Spirit, Ministry
Zech. 4:6; John 15:1–8; Acts 1:8

Date used _____ Place _____

In *Who Needs God,* Harold Kushner writes:

The next time you go to the zoo, notice where the lines are longest and people take the most time in front of the cage. We tend to walk briskly past the deer and the antelope, with only a passing glance at their graceful beauty. If we have children, we may pause to enjoy the antics of the seals and the monkeys. But we find ourselves irresistibly drawn to the lions, the tigers, the elephants, the gorillas.

Why? I suspect that without realizing or understanding it, we are strangely reassured at seeing creatures bigger or stronger than ourselves. It gives us the message, at once humbling and comforting, that we are not the ultimate power.

Our souls are so starved for that sense of awe, that encounter with grandeur which helps to remind us of our real place in the universe, that if we can't get it in church, we will search for it and find it someplace else.

Awe, Creation, Pentecost, Reverence
Ps. 19:1–6; Rom. 1:18–23; 11:34–36; 1 Cor. 2:1–5

Date used _____ Place _____

In the *Pentecostal Evangel,* J. K. Gressett writes about a man named Samuel S. Scull who settled on a farm in the Arizona desert with his wife and children.

> One night a fierce desert storm struck with rain, hail, and high wind. At daybreak, feeling sick and fearing what he might find, Samuel went to survey their loss.
>
> The hail had beaten the garden and truck patch into the ground; the house was partially unroofed; the henhouse had blown away, and dead chickens were scattered about. Destruction and devastation were everywhere.
>
> While standing dazed, evaluating the mess and wondering about the future, he heard a stirring in the lumber pile that was the remains of the henhouse. A rooster was climbing up through the debris, and he didn't stop climbing until he had mounted the highest board in the pile. That old rooster was dripping wet, and most of his feathers were blown away. But as the sun came over the eastern horizon, he flapped his bony wings and proudly crowed.

That old, wet, bare rooster could still crow when he saw the morning sun. And like that rooster, our world may be falling apart, we may have lost everything, but if we trust in God, we'll be able to see the light of God's goodness, pick ourselves out of the rubble, and sing the Lord's praise.

Crisis, Perseverance, Thanksgiving, Trials
Acts 16:22–25; 1 Thess. 5:16–18

Date used _____ Place _____

In *Contemporary Christian Music,* John Fischer writes:

I have a bad habit. When my children tell me about something they've learned for the first time, I often act as if I knew that. Even worse, sometimes I tell them how the same thing happened to me years ago.

When my wife hears something "new" from the kids, her mouth drops open and her eyes widen. It's as if she has never heard this kind of thing before. The kids' faces brighten, and they feel as if they have actually enlightened their mother.

I used to think my wife was just acting and sooner or later the kids would find out and feel lied to. Then I realized it isn't an act at all. Though she may already have experienced what they are trying to tell her, she's never experienced it through them. Their personal "revelations" are entirely new.

It's the same with God. As all-knowing and sovereign as he is, I'm sure he's still eager to hear our prayers because he has never heard it quite the way we say it. We are all unique. We have our own signature attached to all we do and say. Our lives, our experiences, and our faith expressed to him are never old.

God the Father, Mothers, Uniqueness
Matt. 6:8; 1 Peter 3:12

Date used _____ Place _____

Hyatt Moore of the Wycliffe Bible Translators writes:

On November 14, 1983, two American students named David and Ray teamed up to pray for the 40,000 Tira people in Africa. The large group had no Bible in their native tongue.

Two-and-a-half years later, other Christians, Jerry and Jan, joined them in praying daily for the Tira. Then, in March 1990, Jane and Marjeanne wrote to the Bibleless Peoples Prayer Project of Wycliffe Bible Translators, asking for the name of a Bibleless people to pray for. They too began praying. . . .

In August 1990, we heard that Avajani, a young Tira man, was beginning to translate the Bible. Great news! We wrote, telling him of those praying and how he was an answer to their prayers.

"I'm grateful," Avajani wrote back. "I have never known that there are teams praying for the Tira people. It is wonderful news to me. The same year and month when David and Ray started praying, I got saved. When Jerry and Jan began praying, I was accepted for theological studies . . . and now I have finished. Jane and Marjeanne can praise the Lord with me, too! In March 1990, a miracle happened. I met a man (a Wycliffe translator) who was able to arrange for me to study biblical translation principles and linguistics.

"God did another miracle. Many young Tira have become Christians."

Today, seven years after David and Ray began praying in faith, the Bible is being translated for 40,000 new readers.

Although we don't always see the effect of our prayers at the time, God hears and answers.

Bible, Faith, Missions
Mark 11:22–24; Heb. 11:1; 1 John 5:14–15

Date used _____ Place _____

Bill Gates, who is chief executive at Microsoft, is hooked up to the international computer network called Internet. Subscribers to the Internet can send through their computers electronic mail (called e-mail) to other users of the Internet. Bill Gates had an Internet address just like everyone. But then *The New Yorker* magazine published his Internet address. Anyone could send the computer genius a letter. In no time Bill Gates was swamped with five thousand messages. It was more than any human could handle. So Gates armed his computer with software that filters through his e-mail, allowing important messages through and sending other letters to electronic oblivion.

People are limited. They can handle only so much communication and offer only so much help.

God, on the other hand, never tires of s-mail (spirit mail). His ear is always open to our prayers. And he has unlimited capacity to help.

Compassion of God, Help, Trust
Matt. 7:7–11; 1 Peter 5:7

Date used _____ Place _____

In his sermon "The Disciple's Prayer," Haddon Robinson recalls:

> When our children were small, we played a game. I'd take some coins in my fist. They'd sit on my lap and work to get my fingers open. According to the international rules of finger opening, once the finger was open, it couldn't be closed again. They would work at it, until they got the pennies in my hand. They would jump down and run away, filled with glee and delight. Just kids. Just a game.
>
> Sometimes when we come to God, we come for the pennies in his hand.
>
> "Lord, I need a passing grade. Help me to study."
>
> "Lord, I need a job."
>
> "Lord, my mother is ill."
>
> We reach for the pennies. When God grants the request, we push the hand away.
>
> More important than the pennies in God's hand is the hand of God himself. That's what prayer is about.

Devotion, God the Father, Love for God
Mark 12:30; Luke 11:1–4

Date used _____ Place _____

Charles Colson, in *BreakPoint,* tells a story from the childhood of a biologist named Benno Muller-Hill.

One day the boy's teacher set up a telescope to show students a planet and its moons. One by one the students looked through the telescope and said, yes, they could see the planet. Finally one student said, "I can't see anything."

The teacher angrily told him to adjust the lenses. Still the student saw nothing. Finally the teacher himself leaned over and looked. When he stood up, he had a strange expression on his face. He glanced at the end of the telescope and saw that the lens cap was still on.

Just as most of the students saw what they were told to see, many people see the world in the way "the world, the flesh, and the devil" tell them to see it.

Children, Dogmatism
Rom. 12:2; 1 John 2:15–17

Date used _____ Place _____

Daniel Okrent was the founding father of rotisserie baseball leagues back in the winter of 1979 and 1980. Since then the pastime has exploded, with more than two million people involved every year.

The basic idea of rotisserie baseball is that participants act like owners and general managers of a baseball team. Each spring they "draft" players from Major League baseball for their rotisserie team. The player's actual Major League statistics—such as a batter's hits or a pitcher's wins—are used in the rotisserie league to determine which team has the best record. During the season, rotisserie owners continue to make team moves, trading players and adjusting their lineups to see who can have the players with the best statistics.

Most rotisserie owners say they spend between five and fifteen hours a week on the game, watching ball games and sports reports and reading newspapers. Some rotisserie owners get carried away. When Cleveland Indians relief ace Steve Olin was killed in a boating accident during spring training, fanatic rotisserie players called the Cleveland Indians to ask who would replace him in the lineup.

One San Diego doctor called in his player move while in surgery.

Rotisserie inventor Daniel Okrent said he once received a letter from a Maryland woman who blamed her divorce on her husband's love affair with the game. Some have dubbed the wives of the game's fanatics "rotisserie widows."

Whether it is rotisserie baseball, bowling, bridge, or the things of God, where your interest is, there will your time and thoughts be also.

Commitment, Interests, Time
Matt. 6:21; Luke 14:15–35; Phil. 2:20–21

Date used _____ Place _____

Disregard for a moment your convictions about gambling, and take note of something special in this news story.

On Friday, March 29, 1984, Robert Cunningham ate a meal of linguine and clam sauce at his favorite restaurant, Sal's pizzeria, where he had been a regular customer for seven years. His waitress, Phyllis Penza, had worked at Sal's for nineteen years.

After his meal Cunningham made a good-natured offer to Penza. He said she could either have a tip or split his winnings if his number was drawn in the upcoming New York lotto. Penza chose to take a chance on the lottery, and she and Cunningham chose the numbers together.

On Saturday night, Cunningham won. The jackpot was six million dollars. Then he faced the moment of truth. Would he keep his promise? Would he give the waitress a "tip" of three million dollars?

Cunningham, a police sergeant, husband, father of four, and grandfather of three, said, "I won't back out. Besides, friendship means more than money."

Promises are to be kept no matter what the cost.

Friendship, Honesty, Money, Truth
Ps. 15:1–4

Date used _____ Place _____

To protect itself from aggressors, the horned lizard uses some unique defense mechanisms. In the *Smithsonian,* Susan Hazen-Hammond writes:

> When the creature is threatened by a large predator, it runs through an elaborate behavioral repertoire. First, the lizard will hiss and swell its body with air. If that doesn't work, the animal will flatten its body into a dorsal shield and tip it up toward the attacker. The predator may decide that this little animal might just be too difficult to swallow.
>
> When all else fails, however, the lizard's eyelids will suddenly swell shut. A hairlike stream of blood comes shooting out from a tiny opening near the animal's eyelids, to be shot point-blank at the aggressor. The blood must contain noxious compounds because it clearly repels the recipient. Then the eyelids shrink back to normal size, and the horny toad—its own cheeks streaked with blood—will look around with what at least one human observer saw as a triumphant expression.

Like the horned lizard, when we feel we have to defend ourselves, anything can happen. But when we're threatened, God wants us to entrust ourselves to him.

Anger, Defensiveness, Persecution, Suffering, Temper
1 Peter 2:19–23

Date used _____ Place _____

In October 1993, police sharpshooters in Rochester, New York, surrounded a car. In the back seat of the car was a man with a rifle. The police attempted to negotiate with the man. No answer. The police watched and waited. No movement. Finally the police discovered the truth: The armed man in the back seat was a mannequin.

When the authorities tracked down the owner of the car, he told them he keeps the mannequin in his car for protection. "You've got to do this," he said. "With the car-jackings, it helps if it looks like you've got a passenger."

These are dangerous times. Whom do you rely on for protection? A mannequin or the Mighty One?

Angels, Fear, Safety
Ps. 91; 121

Date used _____ Place _____

In 1937 Walt Disney released the first full-length animated movie: *Snow White and the Seven Dwarfs.* Producing an animated movie was a gargantuan task. Disney artists drew over one million pictures. Each picture flashed onto the screen for a mere one-twenty-fourth of a second.

As we watch the movie run at regular speed, it seems so simple. We have no idea all that goes into it.

Our lives are like that movie. God puts infinite thought, skill, and careful attention into every detail. Yet as our lives run at "regular speed," we have no idea how much God's providence fills every single second.

Help, Sovereignty of God
Ps. 139:13–18; Jonah 4:6; Matt. 10:29–31; Phil. 2:13

Date used _____ Place _____

Cliff Barrows has served as Billy Graham's lifelong associate and crusade song leader.

In 1945, before he met Billy Graham, Barrows and his fiancée, Billie, had scraped together enough funds for a simple wedding and two train tickets to a city with a resort hotel.

On arrival, however, they found the hotel shut down. Stranded in an unfamiliar city with little money, they thumbed a ride. A sympathetic driver took them to a grocery store owned by a woman he knew. The newlyweds spent their first night in a room above the store.

The next day, when the lady overheard Cliff playing Christian songs on his trombone, she arranged for them to spend the rest of their honeymoon at a friend's house. Several days later the host invited them to attend a youth rally where a young evangelist was speaking.

The song leader that night was sick, and Cliff was asked to take charge of the music for the service. The young evangelist, of course, was Billy Graham. The two have been partners ever since.

When things don't go the way you plan, God may have plans for you of his own.

God's direction, Plans
Rom. 8:28; Phil. 2:13

Date used _____ Place _____

In *World Vision* magazine, John Robb wrote about an occasion when he saw God's perfect timing.

Robb was in Moscow to teach a seminar at the week-long Lausanne Soviet Congress on Evangelization. While there he met a man named Mirza who was a doctor from Azerbaijan. Azerbaijan is a Muslim region where there were only twenty known converts to Christ. Robb had an opportunity to tell Mirza about Jesus Christ and he wanted to give him some Christian literature. To Robb's dismay he found he had already given away all the Bibles he had brought, but he had one gospel tract left. Robb writes:

[Mirza] showed up again the next day at my hotel room just as I was leaving for the airport. He expressed his appreciation for my friendship, saying that he hoped we could meet again.

I thought, *Lord, what I'd give for a Russian New Testament right now.*

Not ten seconds later there was a knock at the door. The Russian Gideons were there with a whole load of New Testaments. They had just received permission from the hotel management to place Bibles in every room! One of them held out a New Testament, as if to say, "Is this what you wanted?" I handed it to Mirza and we said goodbye.

God obviously had a purpose for Mirza. And when God is at work, there are no coincidences.

Divine appointments, Evangelism, Sovereignty of God
Acts 8:26–39; 2 Cor. 2:12–16

Date used _____ Place _____

In his sermon, "A Purpose Runs through It," Bryan Wilkerson says:

One of the most beautiful movies of [recent years] was *A River Runs through It*, based upon the novel by the same title. The movie told the story of the Maclean family, who lived in Montana early in the twentieth century. The father of the family was a Presbyterian minister—stern but loving. His wife was supportive and nurturing. They had two sons: the oldest, first-born Norman, who tells the story, and a younger son, Paul. . . .

The real protagonist in the story is the river that runs through their part of Montana. That river becomes the focal point of their family life and the catalyst for everything significant that takes place in their individual lives. It was walking along the banks of that river on Sunday afternoons that the father forged a relationship with his young boys—turning over rocks, teaching them about the world, about life, and about the God who made it all. It was the river that the boys ran to after their studies were over, and sibling rivalry and brotherly affection flourished as they fished for trout together on that beautiful stream.

When it came time for these adolescent boys to prove their moxie, they took a death-defying ride down the rapids in a stolen boat. It was on the river that young Paul made a name for himself as the finest fly-fisherman in the territory. When Norman came back from college searching for himself and his roots, it was to the river that he went to fish, alongside his brother.

The Maclean family knew failure and success and laughter and fighting and change and disappointment, but always the river was there. It was the defining force and the spiritual center of that family. Montana would have been just a wilderness; their home, four walls and a roof; their individual lives just sound and fury—if not for the river running through it all.

I would like to suggest that there is a river that runs through the lives of Christian people, and that river is called the Purpose of God. . . .

For the remainder of the sermon Wilkerson deals with the tough questions that people in his congregation were facing after the death of a little girl in the church. As he explains difficult theological concepts, he repeatedly comes back to the image of the river, concluding with the following words:

"Christian, whatever has happened to you in the past, whatever your present circumstances may be, whatever the future might hold, know this: A river runs through it, and that river is called the Purpose of God."

Family, Fathers, God's will, Goodness of God,
Providence, Roots, Sovereignty of God
Jer. 29:11; Rom. 8:28–30; Phil. 2:13

Date used _____ Place _____

Used by permission of the author.

In *The Hiding Place,* Corrie ten Boom writes about a question she asked her father.

"Father, what is sex sin?"

My father turned to look at me, as he always did when answering a question, but to my surprise he said nothing. At last he stood up, lifted his traveling case from the rack over our heads, and set it on the floor.

"Will you carry it off the train, Corrie?" he said. I stood up and tugged at it. It was crammed with the watches and spare parts he had purchased that morning.

"It's too heavy," I said.

"Yes," he said. "And it would be a pretty poor father who would ask his little girl to carry such a load. It's the same way, Corrie, with knowledge. Some knowledge is too heavy for children. When you are older and stronger, you can bear it. For now you must trust me to carry it for you."

And I was satisfied. More than satisfied—wonderfully at peace. There were answers to this and all my hard questions— but now I was content to leave them in my father's keeping.

And so it is that to find peace, we must leave many questions in our heavenly Father's keeping.

Knowledge, Mystery, Sex, Tragedy, Trials, Trust
Deut. 29:29; John 16:12

Date used _____ Place _____

According to writers Kent McDill and Melissa Isaacson, Don Calhoun worked for five dollars an hour at an office supply store in Bloomington, Illinois. He had attended two Chicago Bulls basketball games in his life, and now he was going to his third. When he strolled into Chicago Stadium, a woman who worked for the Bulls organization walked up to him and told him they were selecting him to take part in a promotional event during the game called the Million Dollar Shot.

The Shot came after a time-out in the third quarter. If Calhoun could shoot a basket standing seventy-nine feet away—that means he had to stand behind the free throw line on the opposite end of the court and throw the ball three quarters of the length of the court—he would win one million dollars.

Calhoun played basketball at the Bloomington YMCA but he had never tried a shot like this before. He took the basketball in his hands and looked over at Michael Jordan and the rest of the Bulls. He could see they were pulling for him.

Calhoun stepped to the line and let fly. As soon as the basketball left his hand, coach Phil Jackson said, "It's good." Indeed, the ball went through the basket in a swish. The stadium crowd went wild. Calhoun rushed into the arms of Michael Jordan, and the Bulls players crowded around slapping him on the back.

When Don Calhoun went home that night, he had only two dollars in his wallet, but he would receive fifty thousand dollars a year for the next twenty years of his life.

Sometimes one action, one decision, one moment can change everything for you. So it is when you choose to receive Christ into your life.

Born again, Conversion, Gospel, Repentance, Salvation
John 1:12; 2 Cor. 5:17

Date used _____ Place _____

In April 1969 more than one hundred Black students at Cornell University took over the student union in a militant demonstration for civil rights. According to the Associated Press, they protested "the lack of Black studies programs and what they saw as the university's treatment of them as second-class citizens." Militants smuggled guns into the building and threatened violence.

Some of the most inflammatory rhetoric came from one Black militant named Thomas W. Jones. He said that Cornell had only "hours to live," that he was ready to lay down his life, and that racist faculty and police would be "dealt with."

The takeover lasted thirty-four hours but ended peacefully. When the one hundred militants finally marched from the building, the same Thomas W. Jones was the last to leave. He walked out carrying a rifle and raising a clenched fist.

One month later James Perkins, the president of Cornell, was forced to step down.

But that isn't the end of the story.

Cornell dealt with the issues that concerned the militants. Thomas Jones earned his masters degree from Cornell one year later and helped Cornell organize a Black studies curriculum. He then went into business, working for TIAA-CREF, the world's largest pension fund, with $142 billion in assets. Jones eventually became president of the company. In 1993 Cornell appointed Jones to their board of trustees.

And in 1995 Thomas Jones made the grand gesture of reconciliation. On May 4 in a ceremony at Cornell, Jones endowed a five-thousand-dollar prize to reward efforts on campus to foster "interracial understanding and harmony." Jones named the annual prize after James Perkins, the former Cornell president forced to step down twenty-six years before.

Jones said Perkins had engineered one of the earliest college drives to enroll Blacks. "I simply feel the need to acknowledge," said Jones, "that he was an extremely decent man who had the courage to do the right thing in trying to help America solve its racial problems by improving educational access for minorities."

At the ceremony, Jones and Perkins sat side by side. Jones and Perkins, onetime foes, show that racial reconciliation is possible. And they show us something else: Racial reconciliation is beautiful.

Forgiveness, Prejudice, Race relations
Gal. 3:26–28; Eph. 2:14

Date used _____ Place _____

Johnny Cash once did an album called *American Recordings*. On the album cover is a picture of two dogs. One dog is black with a white stripe. The other dog is white with a black stripe. The two dogs are meant to say something about Johnny Cash.

In an interview with *Rolling Stone*, Cash explains what the two dogs mean. "Their names are Sin and Redemption. Sin is the black one with the white stripe; Redemption is the white one with the black stripe. That's kind of the theme of that album, and for me, too. When I was really bad, I was not all bad. When I was trying to be good, I could never be all good. There would be that black streak going through."

No one is all bad. No one is all good. We are all sinners who need to be redeemed. We all need Jesus.

Grace, Jesus Christ, Perfection, Salvation, Sin, Struggle, Works
Rom. 3:9–26; 7:7–25

Date used _____ Place _____

In his sermon "The Writing on the Wall," William Willimon tells the story of an aggravating funeral at a country church.

The preacher pounded on the pulpit and looked over at the casket. He would say, "It's too late for Joe. He might have wanted to get his life together. He might have wanted to spend more time with his family. He might have wanted to do that, but he's dead now. It is too late for him, but it is not too late for you. There is still time for you. You still can decide. You still are alive. It is not too late for you. Today is the day of decision."

Then the preacher told how a Greyhound bus had run into a funeral procession once on the way to the cemetery, and that could happen today. He said, "You should decide today. Today is the day to get your life together. Too late for old Joe, but it's not too late for you."

I was so angry at that preacher. On the way home, I told my wife, "Have you ever seen anything as manipulative and as insensitive to that poor family? I found it disgusting."

She said, "I've never heard anything like that. It was manipulative. It was disgusting. It was insensitive. Worst of all, it was also true."

Death, Decisions, Receiving Christ
2 Cor. 6:2

Date used _____ Place _____

Don Wyman's chain saw revved like a motorcycle and ripped through a three-foot-thick oak tree. The day was Tuesday, July 20, 1993, in a forest one hundred miles northeast of Pittsburgh, Pennsylvania, and Wyman, a mustached and burly mining company employee, was cutting up a fallen tree. It was about 4:00 P.M., and he was alone in the woods.

When he finished one cut, tragedy struck, say writers Pam Lambert and Tom Nugent. The tree snapped back in his direction and knocked him to the ground. The massive oak landed on his left shin, shattering bone and tearing flesh. Pinned to the ground, Wyman screamed in pain.

He tried to free himself. He still had his chain saw, but he couldn't reach enough of the tree to cut himself free. So he began digging around and beneath his leg, using the saw to chop the hard soil and then scooping the dirt with his hands. Every few minutes he paused and bellowed for help, to no avail.

Then he hit a large rock, too large to dig around or move. An hour had passed since the accident. *I'm going to bleed to death,* he thought.

He weighed his options. He could lie there, continue to call for help, and hope that by some slim chance a person would wander into earshot or that he could survive until his wife figured that something was wrong and sent someone looking for him. He could give up and bleed to death. Or he could do a very scary thing, a desperate measure in a desperate time. He had a pocket knife. Maybe he could muster the strength to amputate his own pinned leg and somehow get back to where someone could help him.

Wyman thought about it for a while, and then made his decision. He pulled the starter cord from his chain saw, wrapped it around his leg, and tied the cord to a wrench. Then he twirled the wrench until it cut off the flow of blood to his shin.

Somehow he amputated his own leg below the knee with his pocket knife.

Now, on one leg, he had to find help. He crawled 135 feet uphill over loose ground to his bulldozer. He climbed in, started the engine, and then drove the slow, grinding earthmover a quarter mile to his Chevy S–10 truck, all the while clutching the wrench-and-starter-cord tourniquet. The truck had a manual transmission, but using a metal file to depress the clutch when he shifted, Wyman was able to drive to a farmer's home a mile-and-a-half away.

When dairy farmer John Huber saw the crazed looking man behind the wheel of the mud-splattered truck and cautiously approached to investigate, Wyman yelled, "I cut my leg off!" Wyman lifted what remained of his left leg as proof and shouted, "Help me! I'm bleeding to death."

Huber ran inside and phoned for emergency help. He then drove Wyman to a crossroads where they met an ambulance. Soon Wyman received the medical care that saved his life.

Don Wyman's leg was dear to him but as he lay bleeding to death beneath the oak tree, he recognized that keeping his leg might cost him his life. We too have things dear to us—sinful pleasures, lusts, and activities—that we do not want to give up. Losing them would be like amputating our own leg or gouging out an eye. Jesus said that we must be willing to repent of even the most precious sins if we want to inherit eternal life.

Choices, Courage, Priorities, Sin
Deut. 30:15–20; Matt. 5:29–30; 7:13–27

Date used _____ Place _____

Each week some three million people read *The National Enquirer*. But big supermarket sales don't necessarily add up to journalistic respect. *The Enquirer* will long be remembered for stories about space aliens and multi-headed humans. Mainstream journalists grumble because the tabloid pays big money to its sources for their tales. And, really, is Vanna White's new baby or the continuing saga of Oprah Winfrey's weight worthy of headlines?

But surprise, surprise, according to *New York Times* writer David Margolick, *The Enquirer* took the prize for reporting in its coverage of the O. J. Simpson case.

"As early as five years ago," wrote Margolick, "*The Enquirer* was on the case. And in a story made for the tabloids, it stands head and shoulders above them all when it comes to aggressiveness and accuracy. . . . With as many as 20 reporters on the case, *The Enquirer* has broken numerous stories."

In his article Margolick went on to list several facts that *The Enquirer* had been first to report. And then to emphasize his point, Margolick listed several erroneous stories that mainstream news agencies had reported but *The Enquirer* had not.

Christians are a bit like *The Enquirer*. God has chosen the "foolish" of the world to shame the "wise."

Election, Gospel, Grace, Ministry, Pride
1 Cor. 1:27–29; 15:8–10

Date used _____ Place _____

In *Moody* magazine, John H. Timmerman writes:

In the back corner of my yard, partitioned by a rose bed and a 40-year-old lilac bush, rests a pile, 8 feet long, 4 feet wide, and 4 feet high—my compost pile. Old-fashioned chicken wire stapled to well-anchored stakes holds it in place. Into it I toss every bit of yard scrap and a heavy dose of kitchen scrap . . . a bit of lime now and then, a good dose of dog droppings, and an occasional handful of fertilizer.

The compost pile burns hot, never smells, and each October yields about 70 bushels of fine black dirt, dark as midnight, moist and flaky, that I spread in the garden. . . . Gardeners call it "black gold." . . . It nurtures 80 roses and a half-dozen beds of perennials and annuals. . . .

Could it be that what nourishes my plants nourishes me?

Timmerman compares his compost soil, which grows rich and fertile as it sits for months, to his life and the need of his soul for rest. Daily life hands us all kinds of things—good and bad—scraps, lime, and even "dog droppings." But as we take sabbath rest, these things are transformed. Godly rest can turn the difficulties of daily life into a rich resource for spiritual fruitfulness.

Fruitfulness, Sabbath, Stress
Exod. 20:8; Mark 6:31

Date used _____ Place _____

Human ashes have been sprinkled into the sky from airplanes and spread over the ocean from ships. But according to the Associated Press, Brian Kelly had something more glorious in mind.

In July 1994 Kelly, who lived in suburban Detroit, suffered complications from surgery on his intestines. Knowing he was soon to die, Kelly told his family what he wanted done with his remains. His request was unusual, but his family granted it.

Kelly's boss, Mary McCavit, at Independence Professional Fireworks shop in Osseo, Michigan, rolled up Kelly's ashes in a twelve-inch-round fireworks shell. On Friday, August 12, at a convention of fireworks technicians near Pittsburgh, they shot that shell into the sky. It trailed two silvery comet tails as it ascended into the night sky, and then it exploded into red and green stars.

If you want to go out in a glorious display, you have to admit, that is pretty spectacular.

But that's nothing compared to the glory that God intends for the bodies of those who believe in Jesus Christ. The glory of our resurrection bodies will far surpass that four-second arc of light and color. Instead of a cannon report, there will be the awesome blare of the trumpet of God and the majestic voice of Jesus calling our bodies from the graves. In glorious resurrection bodies like that of Jesus Christ himself, we will ascend into the clouds and meet the King of Kings whose brightness is like the lightning shining from east to west. For ever and ever, Jesus said, we will "shine like the sun in the kingdom" of our Father.

Body, Death, Easter, Glory
Matt. 13:43; 1 Cor. 15:35–57; 1 John 3:2

Date used _____ Place _____

Poet Elizabeth Goldring developed blindness as an adult. According to writers Ron Kotulak and Jon Van, one day a doctor was testing her eyes with a laser device called a scanning laser ophthalmoscope when Goldring by chance noticed something important. As the laser scanned her eye, she could "see" certain images.

Further experiments were done by Robert Webb, the inventor of the laser device. Goldring found that the laser device was able to project on the retina of her eyes faces and words that she could see.

Based on these experiments, researchers believe many blind people have parts of their retinas that may be able to sense visual information projected directly onto their retinas by a laser.

After the experiments Goldring said, "That was the first time in several months that I had seen a word, and for a poet, that's an incredible feeling."

Just as Elizabeth Goldring could not see without the assistance of this laser device projecting words and images into her eyes, there are many truths we cannot see unless God reveals them to us by his Spirit. We are blind about spiritual things apart from revelation.

Spiritual gifts, Word of knowledge
Matt. 16:13–17; 1 Cor. 2:6–16

Date used _____ Place _____

In 1946 Akio Morita and another man started a new company called Tokyo Telecommunications Engineering in a bombed-out department store in Tokyo, says writer Kevin Maney.

In 1955 Mr. Morita's company made the world's first portable transistor radio. An American company, Bulova, offered to buy the radios at a handsome profit, but the deal troubled Mr. Morita. Under the deal Bulova would sell the radios under their own name.

Morita wanted to establish his own company's brand name. So even though the deal would have brought his struggling company a much needed infusion of cash, Morita decided against the deal, telling the executives at Bulova, "I am now taking the first step for the next fifty years of my company."

Morita's company went on to become one of the greatest success stories in business. Besides the transistor radio, they built the first VCRs and the first compact disc players.

Incidentally, by the time he turned down the deal with Bulova, Morita had already changed the name of his company—to Sony.

In business the choice is often between present and future rewards—with the biggest rewards coming in the years ahead.

To enter the kingdom of God, we must forsake the enticing but small rewards this life offers to gain the reward of life eternal.

Faith, Priorities, Risk
Matt. 6:19–21; Rom. 8:18–25; 2 Cor. 4:16–18; Rev. 2:17; 3:5

Date used _____ Place _____

In December 1994 syndicated columnist Bob Greene told the inspiring story of Rob Mouw.

Rob played on the soccer team in his senior year at Wheaton Christian High School. In the final seconds of a big game against favored Waubonsie Valley, with his team behind by one goal, Rob was dribbling the ball in front of him, running at full speed toward the opponent's goal. Just before he shot the ball, though, he caught sight of the scoreboard. The clock read 00.00. But like any good athlete, Rob shot the ball anyway, and it went in for a goal. The referee signaled that the goal counted, and the game finished in a tie.

The Wheaton fans cheered. The Waubonsie Valley fans cried that time had run out.

Rob had a choice to make. He could say nothing and avoid a loss. After all, it was the referee's job to decide the calls, not his. Or Rob could do what was right.

Rob asked the referee whether the official time was kept on the scoreboard or the referee's stopwatch. The referee said the scoreboard time was official and then ran off the field. Rob went to his coaches and explained that just before his kick, he had seen zeros on the scoreboard clock. Since he hadn't heard a whistle, he kept playing. But his goal was late, and he didn't think it should count.

His coaches agreed, and so they went over to the opposing coaches, explained what had happened, and conceded victory to Waubonsie Valley.

Bob Greene ended his article with this quote from Rob Mouw: "Every time in your life you have an opportunity to do right, you should be thankful. For a person to know what right is, and then not to do it—that would be a sin. To have won the game—I mean, really, who cares? Doing the right thing is more important. It lets you have peace."

But that wasn't the end of the story, writes Kevin Dale Miller. "Sometime later Rob received a handwritten letter from a total stranger that said:

> Dear Rob, I read Bob Greene's wonderful column about you. I love sports and true sportsmen. My faith in our future was renewed and lifted by that column. Never lose your principles. Always stand for what's decent and right. That's what you told us all when you refused the victory!

The letter was signed by former President George Bush.

Doing what's right—it sometimes gets the attention and approval of the newspaper and even former presidents. It always gets the attention and approval of God.

Honesty, Integrity, Sportsmanship, Teenagers
2 Cor. 8:21; 13:8; 1 Tim. 4:12

Date used _____ Place _____

In his book *Ordering Your Private World,* Gordon MacDonald tells how one of his college professors gave him a piece of priceless advice.

Here's how it happened. MacDonald read a paper to a special gathering of students and teachers at Denver Seminary expressing his views on a burning moral issue. To write that paper, MacDonald had cut two of his classes during the day, one of which was the missiology class of Dr. Raymond Buker.

Dr. Buker came up to MacDonald after the special meeting and said, "Gordon, the paper you read tonight was a good one but it wasn't a great one. Would you like to know why?"

MacDonald sensed this would hurt but said yes.

"The paper wasn't a great one," Dr. Buker said as he thumped his finger on MacDonald's chest, "because you sacrificed the routine to write it."

MacDonald writes:

In pain I learned one of the most important lessons I ever needed to learn. Because my time as a Christian leader is generally my own to use as I please, it would be very easy to avoid routine, unspectacular duties and give myself only to the exciting things that come along. But most of life is lived in the routine, and Buker was right: The man or woman who learns to make peace with routine responsibilities and obligations will make the greatest contributions in the long run.

Correction, Responsibility, Self-discipline
Luke 17:7–10

Date used _____ Place _____

Gordon MacDonald writes:

One Saturday morning I sat in our kitchen obviously rattled and withdrawn, and my wife, Gail, was trying to discern what it was that was bothering me. Suddenly, she asked one question too many, and I broke into weeping. Even now, I remember the next two hours vividly because it seemed as if I would never be able to stop the flow of tears. . . .

For the previous two weeks I had minimized my sleep because of busyness; thus I was physically exhausted. I had allowed my schedule to become so packed that I had ignored any times of personal worship; thus I was spiritually empty. In what seemed to be a remarkable coincidence I had presided at two funerals of indigent men who had died on the city streets and whose lives and deaths seemed to me to be so terribly meaningless. The experiences had profoundly affected me. Additionally, I had been reading a then well-known author who was launching an attack on matters of personal belief important to me, and I was not responding well to his logic.

On that Saturday morning I was a dried-out man. My resources were nonexistent. Years and accumulated experience later, I would know better than to get backed into such a corner. But I didn't know that then. It was a difficult way to learn an important lesson about being empty.

Burnout, Emotions, Fatigue, Work
Mark 6:31

Date used _____ Place _____

Used by permission of the publisher.

According to the Associated Press, the North Carolina state medical board suspended the license of a neurosurgeon in Wilmington, North Carolina, after an investigation turned up remarkably casual behavior on his part during brain surgery.

The investigation revealed that in the middle of one surgery, as a patient's brain was exposed, the neurosurgeon left the operating room for twenty-five minutes to go and have lunch. While he was having lunch, no other physician was present in the operating room to care for the patient.

In another case the neurosurgeon told a nurse to drill holes in a patient's head and work on the outer brain even though she was untrained for such procedures.

When a person regularly deals with awesome things, he or she can become too familiar and too casual with them. We must guard against that ever happening with the sacred things of God.

Overfamiliarity, Respect, Reverence
1 Sam. 2:12–17; 1 Peter 1:17–19

Date used _____ Place _____

In 1994 Northwest Airlines offered some unusual round-trip passages aboard one of their planes. Fifty-nine dollars bought a "Mystery Fare" ticket that provided a one-day trip to an unknown American city. Buyers didn't find out where they were heading until they arrived at the airport the day of the flight. Still, the airline had plenty of takers. In Indianapolis fifteen hundred people crowded the airline counter to buy the Mystery Fare tickets that were sold on a first-come, first-served basis.

Not surprisingly, when buyers learned their destination, not all were thrilled. One buyer who was hoping for New Orleans but found he had a ticket for Minneapolis walked through the airport terminal yelling, "I've got one ticket to the Mall of America. I'll trade for anything."

Mystery Fare tickets may be a fun surprise for a weekend vacation, but normally the last thing you want is a ticket to a mystery destination. And one time you never want a Mystery ticket is on the day of your death. You don't want to face eternity uncertain about whether you will go to heaven or hell.

Assurance, Eternal life, Heaven, Hell, Judgment
John 1:12; 1 John 5:13

Date used _____ Place _____

In 1973 Gary Kildall wrote the first popular operating system for personal computers, named CP/M. According to writer Phillip Fiorini, IBM approached Kildall in 1980 about developing the operating system for IBM PCs. But Kildall snubbed IBM officials at a crucial meeting, according to another author, Paul Carroll. The day IBM came calling, he chose to fly his new airplane. The frustrated IBM executives turned instead to Bill Gates, founder of a small software company called Microsoft, and his operating system named MS-DOS. Fourteen years later Bill Gates was worth more than eight billion dollars.

Of Kildall, who has since died, author Paul Carroll says, "He was a smart guy who didn't realize how big the operating system market would become."

In a similar way, people often don't realize how big God's kingdom will someday become. God comes calling with the offer of a lifetime, and we find other things to do.

Appointed time, Excuses, Kingdom of God, Opportunity, Priorities
Luke 14:15–24; 2 Cor. 6:1–2

Date used _____ Place _____

Satan is a schemer who uses all sorts of tricks to lure people into sin. One of his tricks is illustrated by a Chicago-area drug user who became a police informant. As an informant this man's job was to induce other drug dealers to sell drugs to him or an undercover policeman, and this informant was unusually successful.

One of his most successful strategies for duping drug dealers, according to Ted Gregory in the *Chicago Tribune*, was to give them a challenge.

This informant says, "I'd tell them, 'Everybody says they can deliver, but you look a little young; or you look a little old; or you look like a nerd.' Let the people think that they're in control. . . ."

This informant succeeded in duping dealers because he understood their psychology. Satan also understands psychology, and he uses the same scheme. He dupes people into thinking they're in control. He challenges their egos. Only after sin takes its course do people find out that ultimately they are not in control—that they are suckers.

Control, Deception, Ego, Temptation
Matt. 4:1–11; 2 Cor. 2:11

Date used _____ Place _____

Have you ever flown in an airplane and wondered why a full cup of coffee doesn't spill when the plane turns? That's right, no matter how steep is the banked turn—even if the wings are perpendicular to the ground—coffee won't spill, a magazine will drop straight to the floor, and stewardesses will walk upright down the aisle as if the plane were level. And unless you are looking out the window, you cannot tell which way the plane is turning. All because of inertia.

Pilots, too, are subject to inertia. When flying through clouds or fog, which prevent them from seeing the horizon, pilots cannot feel the plane's wings beginning to bank to the left or right. In fact in the early days of flight, pilots followed the myth of instinct: They believed they *could* feel the turn, and when their planes were accidently engulfed in fog or clouds, many banked unknowingly into a spiral dive that ended in a crash. That's why pilot William Langewiesche writes, "Instinct is *worse* than useless in the clouds."

To fly through clouds, pilots must rely on instruments like the artificial horizon. The artificial horizon is a gyroscopically steadied line that stays level with the earth's surface and unerringly indicates when the wings are banking left or right. The artificial horizon revolutionized flying, but when it was first invented, pilots resisted using it. The biggest problem flyers had was belief. They trusted their feelings more than their instruments.

In the Christian life God's Word acts as our primary flight instrument. Our feelings can mislead us, but God's Word tells us the truth.

Confusion, Faith, Feelings
Prov. 3:5–6; 2 Cor. 5:7

Date used _____ Place _____

You just know that some things are going to happen sooner or later.

That's the way it was with Michael Parfit, a writer for *Smithsonian* magazine. For a feature article on the mighty Mississippi River, Parfit rode in a twelve-foot rubber dinghy down the Mississippi from Memphis, Tennessee, to the Gulf of Mexico.

Parfit learned of the incredible power of this giant river. The Mississippi gathers its water from 41 percent of the continental U.S., catching water from Montana to New York. Half a trillion tons of water flow down the Mississippi every year, carrying downstream sixty-three thousand tons of soil a day.

A river this big is a threat to the surrounding countryside. That's why engineers have built levees to pinch the mighty giant and keep it from flooding the farmland and towns nearby. The levees on the lower Mississippi stand, on average, twenty-five feet high and run for 2,203 miles on both sides of the main river and its tributaries.

"As the wall was built over the years," writes Parfit, "people came to live under its protection. They tore down the forest and planted cotton, and the floodplain of the Mississippi became the expanse of farmland known as the Mississippi Delta."

More than eight million people live in the Delta. But at what risk? Parfit flew in a plane over the Mississippi Delta and saw plainly the river's tracks on the land, where it once had flooded the Delta.

"The levee . . . cages the giant, or appears to," writes Parfit. "And no one but birds and an occasional light-plane pilot notices the long sweep of the river's indelible script. What the river has written in the mud again and again is simple: 'Someday soon.'"

Someday soon will come another flood. That's what Parfit warned in February of 1993. Someday soon will come another devastating flood like the ones in 1882, 1927, and 1973.

"People in this valley get a sense everything is totally controlled," one engineer told Parfit. "That's a false sense of security. We haven't seen anything yet in this valley as to what this river can do. We're not in control of anything."

"The river," wrote Parfit in February 1993, "moves brown, swift, unpredictable, enormous, always murmuring 'Someday soon . . .'"

In February 1993 when his article was published, Parfit could not have imagined how right he would be. Only months after the publication of the article, in the summer of 1993, came one of the worst floods in the history of the Mississippi.

God's Word warns that *someday soon,* in a moment, in the twinkling of an eye, Christ will return to the earth, bringing the terrible wrath of God on all who have not prepared their lives for his coming. Nothing can stop him. The wise person gets ready.

Judgment, Wrath
Luke 17:24–37; Rev. 19:11–21

Date used _____ Place _____

Neil Howe and Bill Strauss wrote a book called *13th Gen: Abort, Retry, Ignore, Fail?* about America's thirteenth generation, the people born between 1961 and 1981. This generation (the thirteenth since America's founding fathers) has been the victim of bad luck and bad timing, according to the authors. The thirteenth generation was the first whose mothers took pills not to have children, the first to go through the divorce revolution, and the first to go to school when schools stopped teaching traditional curriculum. As a result they have a strange combination of optimism and pessimism about life.

"They're individually optimistic and collectively pessimistic," says Neil Howe. "I liken them to a group of skydivers hurtling to the ground with only one parachute among them, but each one expects he'll get it."

Is there good reason for such feelings?

The Bible is also marked by a striking combination of optimism and pessimism. Scripture is absolutely pessimistic about humankind's ability to solve the problems of this world. We are hurtling toward the end. But the Bible is absolutely optimistic about the future. Christ is coming again to establish the kingdom of God on the earth. For *everyone* who believes on him, there *is* a parachute.

Busters, Gospel, Hope, Optimism, World
1 Thess. 4:13–18

Date used _____ Place _____

Second Coming

In *Out of Africa,* Isak Dinesen tells this story about her Kenyan cook Kamante.

One night, after midnight, [Kamante] suddenly walked into my bedroom with a hurricane-lamp in his hand, silent, as if on duty. . . . He spoke to me very solemnly, . . . "I think that you had better get up. I think that God is coming."

When I heard this, I did get up, and asked why he thought so. He gravely led me into the dining-room which looked west, toward the hills. From the door-windows I now saw a strange phenomenon. There was a big grass-fire going on, out in the hills, and the grass was burning all the way from the hill-top to the plain; when seen from the house it was nearly a vertical line. It did indeed look as if some gigantic figure was moving and coming toward us. I stood for some time and looked at it, with Kamante watching by my side, then I began to explain the thing to him. . . . But the explanation did not seem to make much impression on him one way or the other; he clearly took his mission to have been fulfilled when he had called me.

"Well yes," he said, "it may be so. But I thought that you had better get up in case it was God coming."

Just in case, be ready. Just in case, be awake. People have been wrong in the past about when he would come, but make no mistake, one day he *is* coming.

Readiness, Watching
Matt. 24:36–51

Date used _____ Place _____

In July 1994 Intel learned that its Pentium processing chip had a flaw. The chip would occasionally give wrong answers for division problems using large numbers. Intel believed this was a minor flaw, something they felt would affect the average user once every twenty-seven thousand years. So Intel decided not to make known the flaw and for months continued to promote and sell the flawed computer chip.

But by Thanksgiving word of the flaw began circulating among computer users. Intel finally acknowledged the problem but tried to downplay its significance. They refused to exchange the flawed chip except in special circumstances. Only when IBM decided to stop selling computers with a Pentium chip did Intel back down and agree to exchange the chip when anyone requested. The Pentium affair was a huge black eye on the image of the company, less because their chip had a flaw and more because they tried to cover it up.

We can point our fingers at Intel, but who of us has not done the same thing? Just as the problem with the Pentium chip eventually came out, so every secret sin in our lives will sooner or later come out. Cover-ups only aggravate the problem.

Confession, Judgment day
Luke 12:2–3

Date used _____ Place _____

Some stories make very clear the importance of self-control.

In December 1993 a thirty-two-year-old man in Buenos Aires died of overeating. At death he weighed 660 pounds. Five days before he died, he ate an entire piglet for dinner, which put him in the hospital's intensive care ward. To carry him to the hospital, doctors had to call the town's fire brigade.

Any appetite that's out of control is dangerous, whether it is the appetite for food, sex, money, or power.

Addictions, Appetites, Depression, Gluttony, Greed
Rom. 16:18; Gal. 5:22–23

Date used _____ Place _____

According to the Reuters news service, on Wednesday, November 9, 1994, Goffrey Mayne of West Haven, Connecticut, pulled his car up to an intersection and thought he noticed a problem with his brakes. He shifted the car into park and got out of the car to check his wheels. With no one at the driver's seat, the car suddenly slipped into reverse and took off backwards at high speed. The steering wheel spun, and the car began to circle round and round in the middle of the busy intersection.

The police and fire departments were called. The car kept circling at high speed, blocking morning rush hour traffic. Almost two hours passed with no end in sight. Finally the authorities devised a plan. They positioned tractor trailers to block traffic. Then they simultaneously drove three front-end payloaders—the type used for earth moving—into the out-of-control car. With the car pinned, firefighters broke the drivers side window, reached in, and turned off the ignition.

The car, as you would guess, suffered extensive damage.

Like a runaway car without a driver, people without self-control are a hazard to themselves and everyone around them. In the end, they are pinned only by painful necessity—debt, divorce, sickness, depression, unemployment, total rejection. How much easier it is to stay at the wheel and thereby save yourself the pain and expense.

Addictions, Discipline, Leadership
Gal. 5:23; 2 Tim. 1:7; 2 Peter 1:6

Date used _____ Place _____

Selfish Ambition

According to the *New York Times*, in the summer of 1994, a Virginia state trooper, who was a member of the bomb squad, and his dog, Master Blaster, became local celebrities when they found bombs at malls in Hampton and Virginia Beach.

That bit of celebrity evidently went to the state trooper's head. A hidden camera later recorded him placing a bomb in a shed that he had been asked to search for explosives. He was arrested and later pled guilty to planting explosives at two malls, a courthouse, and a coliseum. He told investigators he had not intended to hurt anyone. The bombs—a cardboard tube filled with explosives, and pipes filled with gunpowder and nails—never exploded. He said he was simply trying to enhance his image.

Selfish ambition is one of the most powerful—and potentially destructive—motivations we can have. When we are in the grips of selfish ambition, we can rationalize almost anything.

Deception, Image, Reputation
Phil. 2:3; James 3:14–16

Date used _____ Place _____

In September 1994 the Associated Press reported on a demonstration by Indian farmers in New Delhi, India. They were protesting the government of India's plans to import three million tons of Dutch dung to be used for farm fertilizer.

Why? asked Indian farmers. There is no shortage of cows in India. And dung from Indian cows would not be tainted by pesticides.

So in protest, about one hundred Indian farmers rolled six ox carts piled high with top-quality, home-grown dung right up to Parliament. Presumably they got the legislators' attention.

Our dung is better than their dung. That's a claim that resembles the pride of the self-righteous person: I am more righteous than they are.

Arrogance, Salvation
Luke 18:9–14; Rom. 3

Date used _____ Place _____

In the summer of 1993 Colin Powell, then Chairman of the Joint Chiefs of Staff, visited the American troops serving in Somalia. On one day he made a grueling twenty-three stops in twenty hours. "Meeting the troops," said Powell in a *Life* magazine profile, "that's what it's all about."

At one base Powell shook hands with four hundred GIs and posed with them for photographs. A picture accompanying the *Life* article shows one such scene. Surrounded by a sea of troops, Powell has his arms around two soldiers as one of them holds his own camera at arm's length to take the shot.

Why did Powell take time for this in the middle of his heavy schedule? Because he couldn't forget what happened on one visit to the Old Soldiers Home in Washington, D.C. As he went from room to room in the hospital, veterans proudly showed him their faded snapshots taken with their commanding officers. Powell says, "That picture they had taken forty years ago with their general was the high point of their lives."

The high point of a Christian's life is similar. Our relationship to our Lord is what gives us our strongest sense of worth and pride. And unlike a photo opportunity, our relationship with Christ lasts forever.

Jesus Christ, Pride, Self-esteem
Rev. 22:4

Date used _____ Place _____

Businessman Harvey Mackay, who authored the book *Swim with the Sharks*, wrote a newspaper column about the importance of leaders being willing to do any kind of work. As an example of being willing to do anything on the factory floor, Mackay mentioned Philip Pillsbury of the Pillsbury milling family. Mackay wrote:

> The tips of three of his fingers were missing. . . . [That's] the unmistakable mark of a journeyman grain miller, albeit a somewhat less-than-dexterous one. [Philip] Pillsbury had an international reputation as a connoisseur of fine foods and wines, but to the troops, his reputation as a man willing to do a hard, dirty job was the one that mattered . . . and you can be sure everyone was aware of it.

The best leaders see themselves as servants. The people that are greatest in the kingdom of God are those missing the tips of their fingers.

Example, Leadership, Work
Matt. 20:25–28; John 13:1–17

Date used _____ Place _____

Shame

At 3 A.M. on April 5, 1956, newspaper columnist Victor Riesel walked out of Lindy's restaurant in mid-town Manhattan. In his columns Riesel had crusaded for some time against gangster infiltration and corruption of labor unions, and earlier that night he had done a radio broadcast in which he assailed the leadership of a Long Island union. Accompanied by a friend and his secretary, Riesel headed toward his car, which was parked on 51st Street.

Near a theater, according to Lawrence Van Gelder in the *New York Times*, a young man stepped from the shadows and threw liquid into Riesel's face. It was acid. The acid hit Riesel in the eyes and blinded him. One month later doctors told Riesel he would never see again.

Riesel later wrote, "There was no terror at the moment when I knew I had crossed the line into permanent darkness. There was only a sudden feeling of shame. I was afraid that people would treat me too gently or shy away from me as though from a freak. And suddenly, I wondered if I could go on writing and earning a living."

Even when it is undeserved, shame is one of the most painful of emotions. (Victor Riesel overcame his unwarranted feeling of shame. He continued to write a newspaper column that appeared in the New York *Daily Mirror* and was syndicated in as many as 350 newspapers until he retired in 1990.)

Courage, Disability, Overcomers
Isa. 61:7; Rom. 10:11; Heb. 12:2

Date used _____ Place _____

In a book called *All Thumbs Guide to VCRs*, which is a repair guide for amateurs, author Gene Williams begins with a warning. He writes:

> Getting a jolt from the incoming 120 volts ac (120 Vac) is more than just unpleasant; it can be fatal. Studies have shown that it takes very little current to kill. Even a small amount of current can paralyze your muscles, and you won't be able to let go. Just a fraction more and your heart muscle can become paralyzed.

Williams knows that the naive amateur repairman doesn't have sufficient respect for the lethal power of electricity. The amateur knows that a shock hurts but he thinks he can always let go of the wire. It is the paralyzing power of even a small amount of electricity that makes it so dangerous.

So it is with sin. People dabble with sin because they don't fear its power to paralyze the muscles of the soul. Then it's too late. Even when people know a sinful behavior is hurting them and they want to quit, they can't let go. Sin is never safe!

Addictions, Correction, Restoration, Temptation
Matt. 19:16–24; Rom. 7:15–23; Gal. 6:1

Date used _____ Place _____

When people dabble in sin and seemingly get away with it, they gain a false sense of security. They're like swimmers in shark-infested waters.

In an article about the great white shark, which hunts off the coast of central California, writer Tom Cunneff says that sharks return year after year to particular areas and they put a dedicated effort into a single attack. A shark stalks its prey at a favorite location by swimming three to ten feet off the bottom in shallow water (30 to 110 feet), waiting up to three weeks before darting to the surface for an attack. Cunneff described one such attack.

In December, James Robinson, a sea-urchin diver, was killed by a great white off San Miguel Island, near Santa Barbara. Robinson, 42, was doing what he had done hundreds of times before—treading water as he took off his diving gear and placed it aboard his boat. In an instant, though, the activity turned from the familiar to the fatal as the shark shot up from the depths for a swift kill. Two crew members stowing equipment on the boat whirled around when they heard Robinson scream. "A great white bit me," is all Robinson, his right leg nearly severed, could mutter once they pulled him onto the deck. He died a few hours later.

Just as this shark stalked its prey, so does Satan. If you choose to linger in the ocean of sin, you can be sure of this: There is a shark in the waters. And sooner or later . . .

Consequences, Occult, Reaping, Satan, Sowing
Judges 16; John 10:10; 1 Peter 5:8

Date used _____ Place _____

In generations past, smallpox was a much feared disease. It killed hundreds of millions of people and scarred and blinded many more. It was highly infectious, contracted by breathing the exhaled breath of an infected person.

At one time there was no cure for smallpox. During the Middle Ages, smallpox epidemics often raged across Asia, Africa, and Europe. In some wars more soldiers died from smallpox than from combat.

In 1796 an English physician named Edward Jenner developed the first smallpox vaccine, says writer Donald Henderson in the *World Book Encyclopedia*, and the vaccination soon spread around the world. Many countries required by law that citizens be inoculated.

The health effort was a great success. In the 1940s smallpox was completely eradicated in Europe and North America. In 1967 only thirty countries still suffered the ravages of smallpox. The World Health Organization began an aggressive program in Africa, Asia, and South America to completely eradicate smallpox from the earth. Vaccination teams traveled from village to village searching for smallpox cases. In 1970 only seventeen countries still suffered from the disease. In 1978 the World Health Organization announced that the world's last known case of naturally occurring smallpox was in Somalia in October 1977. In 1980 they formally announced that smallpox had been eliminated.

But stocks of the smallpox virus were stored in freezers at the Center for Disease Control and Prevention in Atlanta. In September 1994 a committee of the World Health Organization unanimously voted to destroy the last stock of the smallpox virus on June 30, 1995. In public health's greatest triumph, the smallpox virus would be completely eradicated from the earth, never again to torment humankind.

It's hard to imagine that such a deadly disease could be completely annihilated. It's also hard to imagine a world cleansed of the plagues of sin and death and evil. But God will one day judge the earth, and by the authority of Christ, sin and death and all that is evil will be thrown into the lake of fire. God will create a new heaven and a new earth wherein dwells only righteousness. There will be no more death or tears, for Christ will have won the final victory.

Consummation, Death, Earth, End times, Jesus Christ
1 Cor. 15:24–28; Rev. 20, 21

Date used _____ Place _____

According to the *Chicago Tribune*, on May 9, 1994, a group of fourth graders at Fuller school on the south side of Chicago accused their substitute teacher of sexually molesting them. By that afternoon the school board promised to bring in counselors for the children. By evening the story was all over the news broadcasts.

But the next day police investigators came and interviewed fourteen of the children, and authorities determined the charges were false. Apparently the children made their false accusation because the substitute teacher threatened to report their unruliness.

One radio announcer reported that one child had promised to give classmates a dollar if they would join in the lie.

Speaking to this problem, Jackie Gallagher, a spokeswoman for the teachers union, said, "[Sexual abuse charges] are one of the hazards of the profession—a new one. Kids get sharper. It is akin to putting glue on a teacher's chair twenty years ago."

The teachers union president said that exonerating the teacher doesn't always make everything better. "What usually happens," he said, "when a person is accused of this kind of thing, is they're exonerated by the board publicly but then later, quietly, they're let go."

Slander is a vicious crime that does lasting harm.

Lying, Reputation
Matt. 15:19

Date used _____ Place _____

One of the world's most remarkable artists could put his entire life's work on the tips of your fingers. His name is Nikolai Syadristy, and he is a microminiature sculptor.

What do microminiature sculptors create? Mr. Syadristy has poised three gold camels inside the eye of a needle—along with a pyramid and a palm tree, writes Howard Witt. He has inserted a flea-sized red rose inside a hollowed-out human hair, as if in a vase. On the flat edge of a cut human hair, he has balanced two tiny, working padlocks, complete with keys. He has copied a six-hundred-note musical score on a chrysanthemum leaf the size of a grain of rice.

Microminiature artists must overcome huge obstacles. One sneeze or cough, and months of work can disappear. Static electricity—the spark that comes when you walk on the rug in winter and touch something—is another challenge. "When I was working on the oasis scene," says Syadristy, "I lost two camels because of static electricity. An electrical surge is like a giant catastrophe for these miniatures."

To carve a chess set balanced on the head of a pin or an electric motor smaller than the belly of an ant, Syadristy must wear thick, Coke-bottle-like glasses and peer through a microscope.

There are only five other microminiature artists in the world.

How difficult it is to work with little things! It is through God's perfect control of far smaller details in creation—molecules and atoms and DNA—that he reveals his unimaginable power.

Power, Sovereignty of God
Matt. 10:29–30; Heb. 1:3

Date used _____ Place _____

In his sermon "Finding God in a Busy World," John Killinger tells the story of a woman whose life was transformed by solitude.

Killinger had traveled to New York to preach, and one night he took a walk with one of his hosts on a promenade that over-looked Manhattan. The woman explained the significance of that place to her. She had gone through difficult times since moving to New York several years before. Her husband had left her. Her daughter had been difficult to raise. One night she had walked to this promenade in such pain and despair that she didn't know how she could go on. Says Killinger:

> She sat on one of the benches and looked across the bay at the city. She stared out at Liberty Island in the distance and she watched the tug boats as they moved in and out of the bay. She sat and she sat. The longer she sat, she said, the more her life seemed to be invested with a kind of quietness that came over her like a spirit.
>
> Down deep she began to feel peaceful again. She said she felt somehow that God was very near to her, as if she could almost reach out and touch God. Better yet, she didn't need to reach out. God was touching her. She felt whole and complete and healed as she sat there that evening. It became a turning point in her life.
>
> "Since then," she said, "whenever I feel under pressure at my job or from any personal problems, I come down here and sit on this very bench. I'm quiet; I feel it all over again, and everything is all right."

Solitude uniquely enables us to sense the presence of God.

Peace, Prayer, Presence of God, Problems,
Spiritual disciplines, Stress, Trials
Ps. 46:10

Date used _____ Place _____

In his book *Enjoying God*, Lloyd Ogilvie writes:

One of the most astounding achievements in ophthalmological surgery is the implanting of a lens in a human eye.

After a friend of mine had this surgery in both eyes, and the bandages were removed, he exclaimed, "How wonderful to have new eyes! . . ."

Our hearts have eyes. . . . Before conversion, our "inner eyes" are clouded over with cataracts blocking our vision. We cannot see ourselves, others, and life in the clear light of truth. Nor can we behold God's true nature or see the beauty of the world that He's given us to enjoy. We are spiritually blinded. . . .

Conversion begins the healing of our heart-eyes by removing our spiritual cataracts. We understand what the cross means for our forgiveness, but we still do not perceive all that the Lord has planned for us and the power He has offered to us.

We need a supernatural lens implant in the eyes of our hearts. . . .

Paul calls this lens the "Spirit of wisdom and revelation." . . . The Spirit is the lens for the eyes of our hearts.

> Blindness, Conversion, Heart, Holy Spirit
> John 9; 2 Cor. 4:1–6; Eph. 1:15–23

Date used _____ Place _____

Used by permission of the publisher.

There is a haunting photo by Alain Keler in the October 1993 issue of *Life* magazine. It is of a boy playing a flute. The boy, named Jensen, is only ten years old, but he probably can play some very sad songs. For when you look at his eyes—or where his eyes should be beneath his long, dark bangs—you see only redness, empty sockets. Jensen lives in a charitable institution in Bogotá, Colombia.

Blindness is always tragic, but the cause of blindness in this case only multiplies the sorrow. In the caption next to the photo, Robert Sullivan explains that the boy was likely the victim of "organ nappers." Eye thieves.

When Jensen was ten months old, reports his mother, she took him to the hospital with acute diarrhea. The next day when she returned, bandages covered Jensen's eyes. Dried blood was spattered on his body. Horrified, she asked the doctor what had happened.

He answered harshly, "Can't you see your child is dying?" and dismissed her.

She rushed Jensen to another hospital in Bogotá. After examining him, the doctor gave chilling news: "They've stolen his eyes."

Jensen is somewhat fortunate. He is alive. The organ traffickers usually kill their victims, excise body parts, and broker them to those willing to pay for healthy kidney or cornea transplants.

Organ thieves in Bogotá, Colombia, are not the only ones stealing eyes. There is someone who steals a person's ability to see in an even more tragic way: Satan.

Blindness, Greed, Satan, Stealing
John 10:10; 2 Cor. 4:4; 1 John 2:11

Date used _____ Place _____

Chile is one of the astronomy capitals of the world, boasting three big-time observatories, including the Cerro Tololo observatory with its five telescopes.

Chile is the mecca of astronomers for several reasons. The sky is clear 85 percent of the time. The Cerro Tololo observatory is built 7,200 feet above sea level in the Andean foothills, where there is less air to distort a telescope's view. The region has a natural inversion layer that keeps the air at high altitude stable and the view better. Northern Chile is also directly under the Milky Way, so astronomers can peer into our galaxy for up to eight hours a night, in contrast to five hours at observatories in Hawaii, which is the astronomy capital of the northern hemisphere.

Certain places on earth offer a clearer view of the heavens, and certain spiritual disciplines offer a clearer view of spiritual things. Throughout the history of the church, believers have found that activities such as Bible memorization and meditation, fasting and prayer, solitude and study, celebration and worship, guidance and confession have helped them better see God and his truth.

Devotional life, Prayer, Spirituality
Matt. 6:1–18; 1 Peter 2:2

Date used _____ Place _____

Lionel Poilane bakes the most famous bread in Paris—large, heavy, round loaves that people line up to buy. Poilane's bread is extraordinarily good because even in our technological age he uses old-fashioned ways. He bakes his bread in brick ovens over oak-wood fires using only the finest of stone-ground wheat. Rudolph Chelminski writes in *Smithsonian:*

> Poilane equips each unit with tools and receptacles that, to a large extent, are straight out of the 18th century. Next to each kneading-trough, for example, hangs a bucket for water, instead of the automated faucet common to most bakeries today.
>
> "I intentionally installed a medieval system," he explains as we amble from oven to oven. "In bakery school, students learn to push a button that delivers 60 liters of water at 40 degrees Celsius. I tried that, but then I realized that the push-button just stops them from thinking about what they're doing—it disengages man from his work. With the buckets, the baker has to think about the quality and quantity of each batch of dough. Sixty liters at 40 degrees isn't necessarily right, you see? In baking, everything is a question of variables—the temperature that day, the humidity, the quality of the flour, and the like. There are no absolute rules. A good baker has to be intuitive and adjust. That's why I like to call my buckets a form of retroactive progress."

The writer summarizes, "From the wicker baskets where lumps of warm dough lie in seductive repose, rising as yeast swells their volume, to the long-handled wooden spatulas on overhead racks to the brick and wrought iron of the ovens and the raging fires within them, everything about [his bakery reflects his] loathing for pointless automation and modern trappings." According to this master baker, technology cannot improve on the baking of fine bread.

Neither can technology improve on spirituality. Like the water bucket, long-handled wooden spatulas, wicker baskets, and oak-wood fires, the spiritual disciplines are ancient but effective. They cause us to be sensitive to God.

Basics, Devotional life, Fundamentals, Prayer
Matt. 4:4; Acts 13:2–3; 1 Peter 2:2–3

Date used _____ Place _____

In *Honest to God,* Bill Hybels writes:

Several years ago, I played on a park district football team. During the warm-up before our first game, I learned that I would play middle linebacker on the defensive unit. That was fine with me; my favorite professional athlete is Mike Singletary, All-Pro middle linebacker for the Chicago Bears.

. . . When it was time for the defense to take the field, I stood in my middle-linebacker position, determined to play with the same intensity and effectiveness I'd so often seen in Mike. . . .

The opposing offensive unit approached the line to run their first play. Mimicking Mike, I crouched low and stared intently at the quarterback, readying myself to explode into the middle of the action in typical Singletary style. The battle raged . . . and reality struck with a vengeance. Using a simple head fake, the quarterback sent me in the opposite direction of the play, and the offense gained fifteen yards.

So went the rest of the game. By the fourth quarter I came to a brilliant conclusion: If I wanted to play football like Mike Singletary, I would have to do more than try to mimic his on-the-field actions. I would have to get behind the scenes, and practice like he practiced. I would have to lift weights and run laps like he did. I would have to memorize plays and study films as he did. If I wanted his success *on the field*, I would have to pursue his disciplines *off the field*. Discipline is no less important on the field of Christian living.

Devotional life, Preparation, Success
1 Cor. 9:24–27; 1 Tim. 4:7

Date used _____ Place _____

On January 16, 1995, Rachel Barton, of Winnetka, Illinois, commuted home on the train. Slung over her shoulder was her Amati violin, worth three hundred thousand dollars, on loan from a benefactor. Rachel is a violin prodigy who first appeared as a soloist with the Chicago Symphony at age eight.

The train stopped at the Elm Street station, and as Rachel exited, tragedy struck. Somehow she got caught in the door, according to Michael A. Lev in the *Chicago Tribune*, and the train started moving again: "Barton was dragged beneath the train for several hundred feet before a bystander heard her screams and notified a railroad official to stop the train. The huge wheels severed her left leg below the knee and seriously damaged the right leg."

Rescue workers and two passengers who used their belts as tourniquets saved Barton's life.

Two months and eight surgeries later, Rachel Barton held a press conference. Sitting in a wheel chair, beaming a beautiful smile, and wearing a glowing red dress, she talked of her plans to walk again, and to perform with the violin in the fall. She was already practicing on her violin several hours a day.

"In the years to come," she said, "I hope to be known for my music, not my injuries."

When we face traumatic pain and loss, we have a choice. We can focus on our past or our future, on our injuries or our gifts. Overcomers dream of the "music" they have yet to play.

> Hope, Loss, Overcomers, Pain, Trauma
> Phil. 1:20–22; 1 Peter 4:10–11

Date used _____ Place _____

In *Charisma,* John Wimber writes about a remarkable manifestation of a gift of the Spirit.

I was once on an airplane when I turned and looked at the passenger across the aisle to see the word "adultery" written across his face in big letters. The letters, of course, were only perceptible to spiritual eyes. He caught me looking at him (gaping might be more descriptive) and said, "What do you want?" As he asked that, a woman's name came clearly into my mind. I leaned over the aisle and asked if the name meant anything to him. His face turned white, and he asked if he could talk to me.

It was a large plane with a bar, so we went there to talk. On the way the Lord spoke to me again, saying, "Tell him to turn from this adulterous affair, or I am going to take him." When we got to the bar, I told him that God had told me he was committing adultery, the name of the woman, and that God would take him if he did not cease. He just melted on the spot and asked about what he should do. I led him through a prayer of repentance, and he received Christ.

Repentance, Secrets, Word of knowledge
Luke 12:2–3; 1 Cor. 12; 14:25

Date used _____ Place _____

According to the Associated Press, in the spring of 1994, Sweden's defense ministry determined that a Soviet submarine had violated Sweden's territorial waters. High-tech buoys around Stockholm had detected suspicious noises, and the military began a submarine hunt in the Baltic Sea that lasted several weeks.

This wasn't the first such alert. Ever since 1981, when a Soviet submarine ran aground near a southern naval base in Sweden, the Swedes had been wary of Soviet intrusions.

But the 1994 hunt didn't turn up any lurking submarines, and one year later the military made an embarrassing admission. The noises picked up by the high-tech buoys had been minks and other mammals splashing in the water in search of food. Minks are about the size of a cat and are plentiful in the islands that surround Stockholm.

When it comes to our enemies and our fears, imagination can easily get the best of us.

Demons, Satan, Vigilance
2 Cor. 10:2–5; Eph. 6:10–18

Date used _____ Place _____

In *The Christian Reader,* Robert Duran of Bethany Fellowship Missions writes of his return to one missions station.

Our horses carefully picked their way along the rock-strewn path. Finally, after two hours of travel by truck and eight hours on horses, we could discern the outlines of the small Huichole village in Mexico. We looked forward to seeing friends we had made in this remote village during three years of visits—most of all, Pastor Alfredo.

First to notice our arrival, the dogs and children loudly brought the news to all those indoors. Huicholes are patient and shy, but one woman, Maria Teresa, beckoned us to her door. Her husband, Santo, was sick and wanted to see us. Their low-walled, thatch-roofed house was built of stone with no windows. Santo lay on a bed made of blankets, which hardly raised him off the dirt floor. He greeted us weakly and was caught by a spasm of coughing.

The first time we had met, three years earlier, a villager had led us to Santo, one of their most feared witch doctors. Before we could introduce ourselves, he shook my hand and said, "Robert, I have been waiting for your visit."

Surprised, I asked, "How did you know my name?"

His reply was, "The guiding spirits left me yesterday. They told of your coming and that they could not stay while you were in the village."

Now, after many visits to the village, and to Santo's home, eighteen people had become followers of Jesus Christ.

Today Santo was happy to see us, and he wanted to talk. "Allow me to pray that I might receive Jesus Christ and follow him," we heard him say. Joyfully, we asked if he was willing to confess his sins and receive Christ as Savior. He nodded. Three times I began prayer, but Santo could not get the words out of his mouth. Finally, after we commanded demonic spirits to leave his body, Santo was able to pray.

Just three months later, Santo's wife told us that one morning, Santo had risen from his sleeping mat and asked for food.

She made him tortillas and, as he ate, he told neighbors gathered in his house, "This is my last meal. Tonight Pastor Roberto's God is coming to take me to his house." That night he passed into eternity, a Christian saved and transformed by God's grace.

The kingdom of God is greater than the powers of darkness.

Demons, Exorcism, Occult

Matt. 16:18; Acts 16:16–18; 2 Cor. 10:3–5; Eph. 6:10–20; 1 John 4:4

Date used _____ Place _____

Used by permission of *The Christian Reader.*

According to the Associated Press, in October 1994, agent Steven Sepulveda of the U.S. Secret Service reported that the biggest thief in calling-card history had been caught. The bandit stole more than one hundred thousand telephone calling-card numbers, sold them to computer hackers around the country, who in turn sold them to people overseas, who in turn made more than fifty million dollars worth of free phone calls to the United States.

The alleged thief, who was known as "Knightshadow" to computer hackers, worked as a switch engineer for MCI. He wrote a software program that diverted and held the calling-card numbers that ran through MCI's switching equipment. The Secret Service said this crime was by far the most sophisticated theft of numbers in history and was part of an international ring operating in Los Angeles, Chicago, and other U.S. cities.

Technology advances, but our sinful nature remains the same. Man continually invents new ways to sin, but God's hatred of sin remains the same.

Sinful nature, Ten Commandments
Exod. 20:15; Rom. 1:28–32

Date used _____ Place _____

In *Broken in the Right Place,* Alan Nelson describes a scene from the book *A Layman Looks at the Lord's Prayer.*

The author talks about watching a potter mold a lump of clay. On the shelves in his workshop stood gleaming goblets, beautiful vases, and exquisite bowls. The potter went to an odorous pit in the floor and took out a lump of clay. The smell was from rotting grass, which increased the quality of the material and made it stick better. The potter patted the lump of clay in his hands into a ball. Placing the lump onto the slab of stone with seasoned skill, the potter sat down on his wobbly little wooden stool. Already the master potter could envision the work of art this lump of earth would become. Whirling the wheel gently, the artist caressed the spinning mound. Prior to each touch, he dipped his hands into the two water basins flanking each side of the wheel. The clay responded to the pressure applied by his fingers. A beautiful goblet arose from the pile, responding to each pinch and impression.

Suddenly the stone stopped, and the potter removed a piece of grit. His seasoned fingers detected the unpliable aggregate. The stone spun again, allowing him to smooth out the former lodging of the grit. Suddenly the stone stopped again. He removed another hard object from the goblet's side, leaving a mark in the vessel. The particles of grain within the cup resisted his hands. It would not respond to his wishes. Quickly the potter squashed the form back into a pile of clay. Instead of the beautiful goblet, the artisan formed the material into a crude, finger bowl. . . . When we resist the Master Potter's hand, we run the very real risk of becoming less than we could become.

Character, Discipleship, Growth, Repentance, Sovereignty of God
Isa. 64:8; Rom. 9:19–21; 2 Peter 1:5–9

Date used _____ Place _____

Used by permission of the publisher.

Stubbornness

According to the Reuters news agency, in the fall of 1994, Alberto Gauna, who lived in the northern province of Chaco in Argentina, became so depressed that he decided to take his own life. He took a .22 caliber gun, pointed it at his right temple, and pulled the trigger. The gun fired, but Alberto lived. So he pointed the gun at his forehead and pulled the trigger. The gun fired, but Alberto lived. So he pointed the gun once again at his right temple and pulled the trigger. Again Alberto lived. Again he fired. Again he lived.

With four bullets in his skull, he decided to shoot himself somewhere else. He pointed the gun at his stomach and pulled the trigger. The gun fired, but he remained conscious. So he shot himself again in the stomach, and still he lived!

Finally, thankfully, Alberto gave up. At the time the story was reported, he was in a hospital in serious condition.

Perseverance isn't always a virtue.

Depression, Ministry, Suicide
Rom. 1:28–32

Date used _____ Place _____

Every year for more than a decade, *The Parachutist*, which is the official publication of the United States Parachute Association, has published an article called their "fatality summary." In the article a writer analyzes the factors contributing to parachuting deaths in the previous year.

Parachutists are classified first as students, then after twenty jumps they receive their A license. After fifty jumps, they receive their B license. After one hundred jumps their C license. After two hundred jumps, their D license.

In the 1993 fatality summary Paul Sitter points to an alarming statistic. Fifty-nine percent of all parachuting fatalities were suffered by elite jumpers, those with a D license. A graph accompanying the article shows a dramatic upward spike for fatalities among those with two hundred to one thousand jumps. The line on the graph falls again for those with more than one thousand jumps.

The lesson is clear. Just because a person is mature doesn't mean he or she is invulnerable. Is it possible that some parachutists with between two hundred and one thousand jumps got overconfident?

Overconfidence, Pride, Temptation
1 Cor. 10:12; Gal. 6:1

Date used _____ Place _____

In 1993 the alternative-rock group Pearl Jam enjoyed huge success with its second album, entitled "Vs." It sold 950,000 copies in its first five days, setting a new record. The previous record was 770,000 copies by Guns N' Roses's 1991 album "Use Your Illusion II."

Pearl Jam's lead vocalist Eddie Vedder made the cover of *Time* magazine.

You would assume all this success would make Eddie Vedder feel great about himself. Not so. "I'm being honest," said Eddie, "when I say that sometimes when I see a picture of the band or a picture of my face taking up a whole page of a magazine, I hate that guy."

Success does not guarantee a feeling of worth.

Meaning, Self-image, Self-respect, Significance
Rom. 8:31–39; Gal. 2:20; 1 John 3:1–3

Date used _____ Place _____

World War II brought unparalleled suffering and death to humankind. Experts estimate some fifty-five million people died, among them roughly six million Jews in concentration camps. Families and nations were shattered. Clearly this was a time of great, great evil.

But all was not evil. During the war, medical researchers intensified their efforts to fight disease and infection and as a result made great breakthroughs. Up until 1941, for example, doctors could not reverse the course of infection. "They could do little more than offer a consoling bedside manner as patients sank toward oblivion," writes Stevenson Swanson.

But the war caused England and America to search for a way to mass-produce penicillin, the original wonder drug. Although penicillin had been discovered by Alexander Fleming in 1928, for nearly a decade the medical community had done little with it. "It was dismissed as little more than an interesting microbiological phenomenon."

But as the probability of war increased in the late 1930s, all that changed. Research began in earnest in England for a way to mass-produce penicillin, which at that time could only be made in extremely small quantities.

In 1941 English researchers brought samples of penicillin to America, and a team of scientists began research into mass production in an agricultural lab in Peoria, Illinois. Within four months they found ways to increase the production of penicillin tenfold. The process was licensed to pharmaceutical companies, and production began in earnest.

"For all of 1943, penicillin production in the United States amounted to just 28 pounds," writes Swanson. "The cost of manufacturing 100,000 units was $20, or about $200,000 a pound. In two years, it fell to less than $2 per 100,000 units, and the country produced 14,000 pounds."

The discovery of the fermentation process for penicillin, the world's first antibiotic, triggered a rush by pharmaceutical companies to develop other antibiotics. Selman Waksman of Rutgers University soon discovered streptomycin, which treated tuberculosis. One antibiotic followed another until in the mid-1990s, well over one hundred antibiotics were available.

"Probably more than any other discovery in the history of medicine, the discovery of antibiotics has done the most to improve the lives of humans," said Dr. Gary Noskin, an infectious-disease specialist and professor of medicine at Northwestern University Medical School in Chicago.

Millions of people died in World War II, but out of the war came the drugs that have saved millions of lives and will go on saving lives. Dr. Russell Maulitz, a medical historian and professor at the Medical College of Philadelphia and Hahnemann University, says, "War is the perverse handmaiden of medical progress."

Just as good came from bad during World War II, so God is able to make great good come from the bad events of our lives.

Cross, Easter, Evil, Good from bad, Trials, Trust
Gen. 50:20; Rom. 8:28

Date used _____ Place _____

Has any athlete had more fans than Michael Jordan? Probably not. Even so, Michael Jordan said something surprising about his need for emotional support to columnist Bob Greene. When Greene asked why he wanted his father to be in the stands during a game, Jordan replied, "When he's there, I know I have at least one fan."

Even the great Michael Jordan needs support. Loyal support. How much more do the rest of us need regular reminders that others are behind us—even when we aren't at our best.

Encouragement, Fathers, Loyalty
Rom. 12:10; 1 Thess. 5:14; Heb. 3:18

Date used _____ Place _____

When people are broken emotionally, they need others to support them until they can stand again.

Medical researchers have developed a bone-bonding compound that illustrates the help we can give others.

The chemical compound looks like toothpaste. Once injected into the body, it hardens in ten minutes. In twelve hours it reaches the compression strength of natural bone.

A study in the journal *Science* found the compound virtually identical to natural bone crystals. The compound so closely resembles real bone that the body does not reject it. Weeks after being injected into the body, the cement is replaced by real bone.

According to the Associated Press, clinical trials "show the material has allowed patients to discard casts early—or altogether—and to resume walking more quickly and with less pain."

In the same way, our encouragement enables others to overcome their pain and walk with the Lord.

Brokenness, Encouragement, Ministry, Weakness
Gal. 6:2; 1 Thess. 5:11

Date used _____ Place _____

In *The Wonderful Spirit Filled Life,* Charles Stanley writes:

In water-safety courses a cardinal rule is never to swim out to a drowning man and try to help him as long as he is thrashing about. To do so is to commit suicide. As long as a drowning man thinks he can help himself, he is dangerous to anyone who tries to help him. His tendency is to grab the one trying to aid him and take them both down in the process. The correct procedure is to stay just far enough away so that he can't grab you. Then you wait. And when he finally gives up, you make your move. At that point the one drowning is pliable. He won't work against you. He will let you help.

The same principle holds true in our relationship with the Holy Spirit. Until we give up, we aren't really in a position to be helped. We will work against him rather than with him.

Dependence, Holy Spirit
Gal. 2:20; Eph. 5:18

Date used _____ Place _____

In the magazine industry, the August 1991 cover of *Vanity Fair* is one of the most well known in recent years. Movie star Demi Moore was on the cover. She was pregnant. Rarely do you see a pregnant movie star as cover girl for a fashionable magazine. But Demi's advanced pregnancy wasn't what shocked the country. Standing sideways, one arm wrapped under her stomach, the other wrapped across her bosom, Demi was stark naked.

At *Vanity Fair*'s tenth anniversary celebration in 1993, they paid tribute to "The Cover." In front of its New York headquarters, *Vanity Fair* unveiled a twenty-two-foot topiary of Demi Moore in her famous pregnant pose. She towers twenty-two feet in leafy-green glory.

Vanity Fair has provided the world an unforgettable illustration by picturing the beauty and fame of a human being in a living bush. Like the grass and the flowers of the field, it will wither and fall, while the word of the Lord will stand forever.

Bible, Death, Eternal, Pornography
Ps. 90:10, 12; 2 Cor. 4:16–18; 1 Peter 1:24–25

Date used _____ Place _____

According to the *Chicago Tribune*, a Chicago area woman came home from work on Thursday, April 14, 1983, at 6 P.M., and when she walked into her apartment, she immediately became suspicious. Gasoline fumes filled the apartment. She thought maybe someone had been working there, so she called the landlady and the janitor. They said they had not let anyone in. With the gasoline fumes still strong, she called the police and fire department. The fire department came and inspected her apartment but found nothing.

Finally at 10:30 she prepared to go to bed. In her bedroom she noticed something unusual. There was a strange electric cord running to her bed and a bulge in the center of the mattress.

She again called the police. When the fire department took the mattress off of the box spring, they found a crude, home-made firebomb. Three one-gallon containers filled with gasoline were sitting on top of a hot plate connected to a timer that was set to go off at 3 A.M.

Subtle. Very subtle.

For that woman to be killed by that crude trap, she would have had to be utterly oblivious to everything in her world.

Surprisingly enough, Satan himself sometimes sets traps for us that are just this obvious. Although he can be the most cunning of deceivers, at times he tempts us in ways that are so obvious, so blatant, so brazen, only a fool would lie in that lumpy bed and turn out the lights.

The Bible tells us to run from temptation!

Satan, Self-control, Spiritual discernment
Matt. 4:3–11; James 1:14–15

Date used _____ Place _____

In *Smithsonian* magazine, Michael Lipske wrote an article about carnivorous plants. The Venus Fly Trap is the most famous plant to feed on insects, but there are many others. The Pitcher Plant, for example, uses a sneaky method to attract its prey— a method that quickly reminds us of the methods of Satan.

Often this plant is brightly colored, mimicking flowers. Sometimes a trail of nectar-secreting glands starts at ground level and leads up the outside of the leaf, summoning ants from the ground to the trap above. Says Lipske:

> The hungry ant or other potential meal is lured to the mouth of the trumpet, so crowded with nectar glands it may be wet. But below this mother lode of sugar, the interior of the pitcher tube is waxy and slick. This is the start of the plant's slippery slope, where victims lose their footing and slide into the increasingly narrow tube. Down inside, the inner wall of the leaf is lined with glands that secrete digestive enzymes, which trickle down and collect in the bottom of the trap. The insect slips lower, to where the surrounding wall is lined with down-ward-pointing hairs that discourage exit. In some species, the bottom fluid contains an ingredient to stun the struggling captive. There may even be a wetting agent that helps soak and drown the victim.

Satan is the master deceiver. He sugarcoats the way to ruin with illicit pleasure. Once a person falls into the trap, Satan makes it extremely hard to escape. He stuns the victim. Then, alas, he digests the victim's soul.

Pleasure, Satan, Sin
1 Cor. 10:13; James 1:14–15

Date used _____ Place _____

In *The Christian Reader,* Lynn Austin writes:

The artificial lures fishermen use look so phony, it astonishes me that any fish would fall for them: shiny metallic and gaudy plastic, hot pink and neon colors in stripes and spots.

Satan knows what he can use to dazzle and distract me. After more than 10 years of introducing myself as "just a housewife," my enemy dangled before me the lure of a "real job" with a paycheck and prestige. To boost my flagging self-esteem, I snapped at the bait and signed a contract before prayerfully considering the consequences to our family life.

Within a few months, I knew I had made a mistake. Early morning meetings forced me to leave the house while my children were still asleep. Afternoon conferences that dragged on and on turned them into latchkey kids.

The demands of the job did not line up with my talents and interests. As the work pressures and the laundry piled up, I missed my daily quiet times with the Lord, my friends at Bible study, and my daughter's Mother's Day program at school.

When my contract expired a year later, I gratefully resigned. I had learned a hard lesson: not to be distracted by fancy lures that make me forget the things that really matter.

Contentment, Distractions, Family, Mothers
1 Cor. 10:13; 1 Tim. 6:6, 9; James 1:13–14

Date used _____ Place _____

Used by permission of the author.

Writer and speaker Joni Eareckson Tada was paralyzed from the neck down in a diving accident. In her book *Secret Strength,* Joni wrote about facing temptation.

I was in my late twenties, single, and with every prospect of remaining so. Sometimes lust or a bit of fantasizing would seem so inviting—and so easy to justify. After all, hadn't I already given up more than most Christians just by being disabled? Didn't my wheelchair entitle me to a little slack now and then?

Joni asks her readers:

When God allows you to suffer, do you have the tendency to use your very trials as an excuse for sinning? Or do you feel that since you've given God a little extra lately by taking such abuse, He owes you a "day off"?

Joni Eareckson Tada teaches us that there is no excuse—not suffering, not great sacrifice, not even paralysis—for indulging impurity in our hearts.

Heart, Purity, Rationalization, Suffering
1 Cor. 10:13

Date used _____ Place _____

Thanksgiving

In the Chilean village of Chungungo water is nearly as valuable as precious metal. The region is arid and parched, forcing the village to truck in fresh water over dirt roads from miles away. Until recently the average person could afford a mere four gallons a day (compare that to the average American who uses ninety gallons a day), and buying even that meager amount soaked up 10 percent of household incomes. In Chungungo bathing was a luxury.

But then scientists experimented with an ingenious new system for obtaining water. The 330 residents of Chungungo now drink water—the freshest they have ever tasted—from high above, atop nearby El Tofo mountain. Under the direction of Dr. Robert Schemenauer, a Canadian cloud physicist, workers hung on eucalyptus poles a "wall" of finely woven propylene nets, each the size of eight queen-size bed sheets sown together. Seventy-five such nets sift the clouds that sweep in incessantly from the Pacific Ocean.

A close look at the plastic nets reveals propylene fibers meshed in tiny triangles. Like dew collects on grass, infinitesimally small water particles from fog collect on these fibers. Ten thousand such water particles must coalesce to produce one drop of water the size of a tear. Still, each water net collects forty gallons of water a day. The seventy-five nets on El Tofo sift a total of three thousand gallons daily from the drifting clouds and fog.

Sometimes our lives feel as dry and parched as the rocky soil around Chungungo, where only shrubs and cactus grow. What we need are spiritual water nets. Few things will flood the reservoirs of our soul like giving thanks to God.

Desert, Holy Spirit, Praise, Refreshment, Thirst
2 Chron. 5:13–14; Eph. 5:20; 1 Thess. 5:18

Date used _____ Place _____

A wine company advertisement in *Newsweek* magazine read, "The earth gives us wonderful grapes. The grapes give us wonderful wine. The wine wins us lots of new friends. Thank you, earth."

How easy it is to give credit and thanks to everything or everyone but the real source of all our blessings!

Creator, Idolatry, Worship
Rom. 1:21

Date used _____ Place _____

Dieters sometimes feel that just *thinking* about food adds inches to their waistline. Dr. Alan P. Xenakis, author of *Why Doesn't My Funny Bone Make Me Laugh?*, says dieters may be right. In certain people, thinking about food increases their insulin level, which makes them feel hungry. Thinking about food doesn't actually add pounds, but an increased appetite may!

Our thoughts stimulate other appetites as well, appetites that can lead to sin. To control our conduct, we first must control our thoughts.

Desires, Self-control, Temptation
James 1:14–15

Date used _____ Place _____

According to the *Chicago Tribune*, in the early 1980s Ed Greer had a good white-collar job with Hughes Aircraft in El Segundo, California. Nevertheless he was miserable. He hated his work and he was feeling pressure from his wife and father. At one point he told a coworker, "Never become too good at something you hate. They'll make you do it the rest of your life."

Greer wasn't willing to do that, and on September 10, 1981, he disappeared. Without telling anyone his plans, he got on a plane and flew to Ft. Lauderdale, Florida. There he lived on the beaches and fixed boat engines. After a while he assumed someone else's name and moved to Houston, Texas, getting a regular job with a small oil exploration firm.

Meanwhile his wife divorced him in absentia. In an odd twist, Greer became somewhat of a fantasy hero to some yuppies who felt trapped in corporate America. Some said they wished they had the guts to do what he did. His former coworkers at Hughes Aircraft even began holding annual celebrations in his memory, with many wearing Ed Greer masks.

Finally in October of 1988, seven years after Greer abandoned his family and career, the FBI caught up to him.

In an interview, the forty-year-old Greer tried to explain his actions: "I felt trapped. I didn't like my life."

Many people can identify with him. Many feel trapped, under too much pressure, in circumstances they just don't like. Many wonder how to escape. But God has a different answer.

Career, Freedom, Fulfillment, Joy, Peace, Stress
John 16:33; Acts 16:22–34; 2 Cor. 1:3–11

Date used _____ Place _____

In January 1993 the Galeras volcano, located in Colombia, South America, suddenly erupted. One week later a geologist, Dr. Fraser Goff, was sampling gas vents in a canyon west of the volcano summit. The guide who was with him jokingly said, "Do you want to look at some gold?"

Dr. Goff picked up some of the rocks and later cut them into thin slices. He found that there was real gold in the rocks, quite a bit of gold. The naked eye could see tiny gold nuggets in the slices.

This was the first time scientists had detected visible gold particles in an active volcano. More than a year later Dr. Goff announced that the Galeras volcano, which remained active, was spewing more than a pound of gold each day into the atmosphere and depositing forty-five pounds of gold a year into the rocks lining its crater. He explained that magma from inside the earth has many components, including gold, and estimated that there is a gold vein at the base of the volcano that is at least ten feet wide.

Just as the ultra high heat and pressure of a volcano can bring gold from below the surface of the earth, the pressure and fiery trials of our lives bring forth spiritual gold. If we draw close to God during difficult times, we find the gold of increasing faith, character, wisdom, and nearness to God.

Character, Faith, Stress
Rom. 5:2–5; James 1:2–4

Date used _____ Place _____

The relationship between a movie actor and a director can make or break a movie. A *USA Today* film critic writes, "In some directors' hands, an actor remains a lump of coal. In others, that same performer will metamorphose into a shining diamond onscreen."

She says Katharine Hepburn did her greatest films with director George Cukor. When Hepburn matched up with a different director, Stuart Millar, her movies suffered.

John Wayne did fifteen memorable movies with director John Ford, but the luster left when he worked with John Huston.

Cary Grant was at his best with director Howard Hawks but couldn't bear to watch his own performance in *Arsenic and Old Lace,* which he did with director Frank Capra.

What is the key to a consistently winning pair? Richard Brown, professor of cinema studies at New York's New School for Social Research, says, "It is only about one thing—trust. A director must trust that an actor has the character inside him or her and that it is within an actor's range. An actor must trust a director with his performance, his work and his image onscreen."

Trust is also at the heart of our relationship with the Divine Director, Jesus Christ. Christ has absolute confidence that by his Spirit he can make us into something glorious. The only question is, Do we trust him to bring out what is best in us?

Christlikeness, Discipleship, Growth
John 8:31–32; Rom. 8:28; James 1:2–4

Date used _____ Place _____

In *Living by God's Surprises,* Harold Myra writes:

My pastor, Bob Harvey, tells how early in his ministry a close friend died. In an effort to comfort the widow, also a close friend, Bob shared all his seminary textbook explanations of how and why God might have let this happen. But the woman rebuked him lovingly. "I don't need a God like that," she said. "I don't need to understand all this. What I need is a God who is bigger than my mind."

Counsel, Crisis, Death, God's wisdom, Pain
Prov. 3:5–6; Rom. 8:28

Date used _____ Place _____

Not many people enjoy going to the doctor, but according to Reuters, in 1994, one London accountant took that to an extreme. The sixty-three-year-old man knew he needed bladder surgery but he could not overcome his fear of doctors and hospitals. So he self-reliantly did what had to be done: He tried to perform the surgery on himself. Tragically he got an infection from the self-surgery and later died. The coroner said, "Unfortunately, [his] drastic remedy went wrong. A simple operation would have solved the problem."

Just as this man didn't trust doctors or hospitals, many people don't trust God. In their self-reliance, they destroy themselves.

Fear, Independence, Salvation, Self-reliance
Prov. 3:5–6; 28:26; Jer. 17:5–8

Date used _____ Place _____

Anyone who has lived or worked in a skyscraper knows tall buildings sway in the wind. There's no danger; the engineers know it will happen, but the sway is uncomfortable for people inside. When engineers and architects designed Citicorp Center in New York, they decided to do something about it.

At the top of the fifty-nine story building, they installed a machine called a tuned mass damper. The machine, writes Joe Morgenstern in *New Yorker* magazine, "was essentially a four-hundred-and-ten-ton block of concrete, attached to huge springs and floating on a film of oil. When the building swayed, the block's inertia worked to damp the movement and calm tenants' queasy stomachs."

When the winds of life gust around us, there is a stabilizing force in the heart of every believer that calms his or her fears. It is trust in God.

Faith, Fear, Stability, Trials, Trouble
Ps. 46:1–2; Prov. 3:5–6; Mark 4:35–41

Date used _____ Place _____

In the late 1970s Hispanic writer Victor Villasenor decided it was time to write his big book. He envisioned a book that would inspire Hispanics, who he felt were desperately in need of heroes.

He heavily researched his family's story, traveling to Mexico, interviewing family members, corroborating stories, checking and rechecking details. The story, which he titled *Rain of Gold*, took him twelve years to write and filled 3,200 manuscript pages.

With a great sense of satisfaction and anticipation he sent the manuscript to his publisher. Sometime later he received shocking news. The publisher intended to publish his book as a fictional novel called *Rio Grande*. Villasenor was outraged.

The publisher had already given Villasenor seventy-five thousand dollars as an advance for the hardcover rights to the book. The book had the makings of a big seller. It was already set up as an alternative selection for the Book-of-the-Month Club.

Villasenor didn't care about all of that. He cared about giving his people a true story that would inspire them for hundreds of years to come. Says Villasenor, "Until a human being does it, we don't know if it's possible. And not knowing if it's possible kills us. That's why it has to be real people that did these things. It stretches human reality."

So Villasenor traveled to New York and shocked the publishing world by buying back the rights to the book. He then sold the book to a small university press for an advance of fifteen hundred dollars. That cost him big money and massive exposure, but it insured that the book would bear the original title *Rain of Gold* and be published as a true story rather than fiction.

Villasenor shows us that pursuing our vision of what is truly valuable is often done at a steep price.

Sacrifice, Truth, Vision
Matt. 16:23–26

Date used _____ Place _____

According to United Press International, as the Vietnam war was nearing its end, a nightmare began for the family of private first class Alan Barton. Barton was killed by a land mine just outside his base in Vietnam. The army was unable to identify the remains. Meanwhile Barton was unaccounted for. Somehow the officers in charge did not see the relationship between those two events, and the army classified Barton as a deserter.

The family, of course, was devastated. Having your son labeled a deserter is a shame for any parents to endure but much more for this family—Barton's father was a twenty-year army veteran.

Alan Barton's mother did not believe her son had deserted. She insisted on his innocence. For thirteen years her son's unidentified remains lay in a military morgue in Hawaii as she fought to clear his name. Finally the army rechecked the morgue records, and this time they correctly identified Alan Barton's remains.

In February 1983 the army honored the soldier it had wronged. They gave Alan K. Barton a full military funeral. Soldiers sounded a twenty-one-gun salute, and a bugler played taps. Barton's mother wept into a tightly folded U.S. flag that moments before had draped her son's silver coffin.

In this world, even heroes may be wrongly incriminated. But just as this soldier's name was cleared and honored, so God promises to vindicate his servants. One day, either in this world or at the final judgment, the truth will come out. The twenty-one-gun salute will be given. The bugle will sound. The flag will be presented. And your name will be vindicated.

Name, Reputation, Slander
Ps. 135:14

Date used _____ Place _____

God has given certain creatures amazing capabilities. The chameleon, for example, shows uncanny accuracy in nabbing bugs with its tongue. Scientists have recently found out why, says Reuters. Chameleons have telephoto eyes.

According to Matthias Ott and Frank Schaeffel of the University Eye Hospital in Tübingen, Germany, the lizards have eyes that work like the telephoto lens on a camera. That requires a positive and negative lens. All other animals in the world have only a positive, convex lens. This is the first discovery of a creature that also has a negative, concave lens. The two lenses give the chameleons super-vision.

Being able to see in ways that others do not often makes the difference between success and failure.

Creation, Goals, Spiritual discernment, Success
2 Kings 6:8–23; 1 Cor. 2:6–16; Eph. 1:17–18

Date used _____ Place _____

According to the *Chicago Tribune*, on May 17, 1987, an Iraqi F–1 Mirage aircraft fired two Exocet missiles at the Navy frigate *USS Stark,* which was patrolling in the Persian Gulf.

The *Stark* was equipped with radar systems to detect such missiles in the air. In the nerve center of the ship was the electronic warfare operator, a man who monitored these systems. If a missile was fired at the ship, he would be warned in two ways. An audible alarm would sound and a visual symbol would appear on the radar screen.

Nevertheless, without warning the Exocet missiles slammed into the side of the *USS Stark* just above the waterline, tearing a ten-foot hole in the ship and killing thirty-seven American sailors.

To learn what went wrong, the House Armed Services Committee launched an official investigation. After visiting the ship and talking to the crew, they reported that the tragedy had probably not resulted from equipment failure. Rather the cause was human error or omission on the part of several people. One was the electronic warfare operator in the ship's nerve center.

The report said, "The operator indicated that he had turned off the audible alarm feature because too many signals were being received that were setting off the alarm, requiring actions that distracted him from performing other signal analysis."

Then with the audible alarm off, according to the investigators, he may have been distracted at the time when the visual signals appeared on the radar screen.

Warning signals are usually an irritating interruption, but we turn them off at our peril.

End times, Preaching, Second coming
Matt. 24:42; 1 Thess. 5:1–8

Date used _____ Place _____

When New York's Citicorp tower was completed in 1977, it was the seventh tallest building in the world. Many structural engineers hailed the tower for its technical elegance and singular grace. The tower was notable for its sleek aluminum sides and provocative slash-topped design. The structural engineer who designed the steel superstructure was William J. LeMessurier, who not long after the building was completed was elected into the National Academy of Engineering, which is the highest honor his profession bestows.

But according to Joe Morgenstern in *New Yorker* magazine, one year after the building opened, LeMessurier came to a frightening realization. The Citicorp tower was flawed. Without LeMessurier's approval, during construction the joints in the steel superstructure had been bolted, which is a common and acceptable practice but does not make for as strong a joint as welding does. What made that a critical problem, though, was that in LeMessurier's calculations he had not taken into account the extra force of a nonperpendicular wind.

He now calculated that the joint most vulnerable to such winds was on the thirteenth floor. If that joint gave way, the whole building would come tumbling down. He talked with meteorologists and found that a wind strong enough to buckle that crucial joint came every sixteen years in New York.

LeMessurier weighed his options. If he blew the whistle on himself, he faced law suits, probable bankruptcy, and professional disgrace. He gave a fleeting thought to suicide but dismissed that as the coward's way out. He could keep silent and hope for the best. But lives were at stake.

So he did what he had to do. He informed all concerned. City and corporate leaders faced the problem in a professional manner, and plans were drawn to strengthen the joints by welding steel plates to them. Contingency plans were made to ensure people's safety during the work, and the welding began in August of 1978.

After the work was completed three months later, the building was strong enough to withstand a storm of the severity that hits New York only once every seven hundred years. In fact it was now one of the safest structures ever built.

The repairs cost millions of dollars. Nevertheless LeMessurier's career and reputation were not destroyed but enhanced. One engineer commended LeMessurier for being a man who had the courage to say, "I got a problem; I made the problem; let's fix the problem."

You may come to a point where you realize your life is like that flawed building. Although by all appearances you are strong and successful and together, you know you have points of weakness that make you vulnerable to collapse. What do you do?

You come clean, get help, and get fixed.

Accountability, Addictions, Appearance, Confession,
Failure, Reputation, Sexual sin
2 Sam. 12:1–25; 1 Cor. 10:12–13; James 5:16; 1 John 1:9

Date used _____ Place _____

John Templeton, who founded the Templeton Growth Fund, held his company's first annual business meeting forty years ago in the dining room of the home of a retired General Foods executive. The company had only one part-time employee and one shareholder.

Forty years later, the Templeton Funds have more than six hundred employees and thirty-six billion dollars in assets. If you had invested ten thousand dollars in the company forty years ago, you would now have three million dollars.

What has been John Templeton's basic stock market strategy? Gobble up stock market bargains. He buys the stock of good companies that for one reason or another other investors hate. In the 1930s he borrowed ten thousand dollars and bought the 104 stocks that traded for less than one dollar on the New York Stock Exchange. He made a killing.

Wherever you find success, you usually find someone who has discovered an effective principle or idea and worked it to perfection.

Money, Saving, Success
Prov. 8:12–21; 24:5

Date used _____ Place _____

To better understand the human body, in 1994, researchers made available a new computer tool called "The Visible Man." The Visible Man consists of almost two thousand computer images.

To produce the images, scientists at the University of Colorado Health Sciences Center took a man's body that had been willed to science and took CAT scans, X rays, and MRI images of it. Then they embedded the body in gelatin. They froze it, sliced it crosswise into 1,800 millimeter-thin sections, and digitally photographed each cross section.

Medical students can look at The Visible Man from any angle, call up an image of any cross section they desire, rotate the images, and put them back together again.

What The Visible Man does for the body, the Word of God does for the soul. God's Word pictures the inner person—our motives, priorities, thoughts, and sins.

Heart, Inner healing, Inner person, Judgment, Motives, Truth
John 17:17; 2 Tim. 3:16–17; Heb. 4:12–13

Date used _____ Place _____

"If a man will not work, he shall not eat." That may sound hard, but the wisdom of that Scripture is seen in the story of one New York man.

According to the Associated Press, this thirty-six-year-old resident of New York was quoted as saying, "I like to live decent. I like to be clean." Nothing wrong with that; the only problem was he didn't like to work. So he found other ways to satisfy his cultured tastes.

He would walk into a fine restaurant, order top cuisine and choice liquor, and then when the check arrived, shrug his shoulders and wait for the police. The sometimes homeless man actually wanted to end up in the slammer, where he would get three meals a day and a clean bed. He has pled guilty to stealing a restaurant meal thirty-one times. In 1994 he served ninety days at the Rikers Island jail for filching a meal from a café in Rockefeller Center.

New York taxpayers have paid more than a quarter of a million dollars over five years to feed, clothe, and house one lazy man.

Laziness, Responsibility, Stealing
Eph. 4:28; 2 Thess. 3:6–15

Date used   Place _____

According to the *Chicago Tribune*, on March 3, 1995, a thirty-eight-year-old man who was walking to his temporary job at a warehouse in Rosemont, Illinois, tried to get there by cutting across eight lanes of the Tri-State Tollway. After he crossed the four northbound lanes, however, the wind blew off his hat. The hat flew back across the northbound lanes, and he chased it. There a semi-trailer truck struck and killed him.

A person can lose everything by chasing after nothing.

Backsliding, Choices, Distractions, Eternal, Money,
Priorities, Temporal, Values
Judges 16; Matt. 19:16–24; Heb. 12:1; 1 John 2:15–17

Date used _____ Place _____

In *A World of Ideas,* Bill Moyers quotes writer Jacob Needleman:

> I was an observer at the launch of Apollo 17 in 1975. It was a night launch, and there were hundreds of cynical reporters all over the lawn, drinking beer, wisecracking and waiting for this 35-story-high rocket.
>
> The countdown came and then the launch. The first thing you see is this extraordinary orange light, which is just at the limit of what you can bear to look at. Everything is illuminated with this light. Then comes this thing slowly rising up in total silence because it takes a few seconds for the sound to come across. You hear a "WHOOOOOSH! HHHHMMMM!" It enters right into you. You can practically hear jaws dropping. The sense of wonder fills everyone in the whole place as this thing goes up and up. The first stage ignites this beautiful blue flame. It becomes like a star, but you realize there are humans on it. And then there's total silence.
>
> People just get up quietly, helping each other up. They're kind. They open doors. They look at one another, speaking quietly and interestedly. These were suddenly moral people because the sense of wonder, the experience of wonder, had made them moral.

Those who have worshiped our wondrous God in spirit and in truth know the feeling. Worship is life changing.

Cynicism, Fear of God, Morals, Wonder
Exod. 20:20; Matt. 17:1–13; Rev. 1:12–18

Date used _____ Place _____

A lightning bolt travels about one hundred thousand miles a second and can reach as far as ten miles, says William R. Newcott in *National Geographic*. Lightning pulses with hundreds of millions of volts of electricity. At the instant lightning strikes, it carries more electricity than all the generators in America could produce. The peak temperature in the lightning channel reaches fifty-five thousand degrees Fahrenheit.

But all that power and heat last for only a moment. The fifty-five-thousand-degree heat lasts for only millionths of a second. The visible flash comes and quickly goes.

Like lightning, God's anger "lasts only a moment, but his favor lasts a lifetime" (Ps. 30:5).

Anger, Judgment
Ps. 30:5; 1 Peter 4:17

Date used _____ Place _____

On August 7, 1994, a 5,200-horsepower locomotive pulled twenty-four cars from Chicago to Fort Wayne, Indiana, and back. On board the train were 846 passengers. The passengers weren't in a hurry to reach their destination, though, because their interest was not in travel per se but in the train. Most were members of the National Historical Railway Society.

Powering this train was a Class J, No. 611 steam locomotive. Steam locomotives may sound very old fashioned but they are very powerful. In fact some of the old steam locomotives were more powerful than three modern diesel locomotives.

The heart of their power, of course, is steam. Steam "is water turned to gas," writes Kate Eaton.

You may think you see it above your whistling tea kettle or on your bathroom mirror, but that's not it. Steam is the clear vapor between the hot water and the visible mist. As it forms, at 212 degrees Fahrenheit, it expands to take up much more space than its liquid state. This explosive expansion, harnessed in a giant locomotive, is what powered 250-ton engines pulling 20 or more railcars through the Blue Ridge Mountains, across the Great Plains and over the deserts of the west. "It's a powerful force," said Robert Pinsky, of the Railway Society.

Just as steam gives power to a locomotive, so zeal gives power to a believer. The more we boil with zeal for Christ, the more power we have for service.

Complacency, Ministry, Passion, Service
John 2:17; Rom. 12:11

Date used _____ Place _____

Notes

(Referenced by *illustration* number.)

1. Luaine Lee, "Great Scot," *Chicago Tribune*, 1 August 1993, sec. 5, p. 3.
2. Bill Powell, "Busted!" *Time* (13 March 1995), 37–47.
"Losing His Barings," *People* (13 March 1995), 50.
3. John Huffman, "Marketplace Christianity," *World Christian* (July/August 1994), 25.
4. "Mixed-up Bus Driver from Motor City Ends Day Nearer Mackinac," *Chicago Tribune*, 8 February 1995, sec. 1, p. 3.
5. "A Perfect Squelch," *Reader's Digest* (September 1990), 82.
6. Otto Friedrich, "I Have Never Been a Quitter," *Time* (2 May 1994), 47.
7. Frederick Buechner, *Wishful Thinking* (San Francisco: Harper & Row, 1993).
8. Eric Zorn, "In Traffic Disputes, Turn Away and Live," *Chicago Tribune*, 8 November 1994, sec. 2, p. 1.
9. "Philadelphia, New York Rank 1–2 in Survey of Hostile Communities," *Chicago Daily Herald*, 14 May 1994, sec. 1, p. 3.
10. Philip Elmer-Dewitt, "Fighting Noise with Antinoise," *Time* (4 December 1989), 94.
11. Debbie Becker and Roscoe Nance, "Cyclist to Get Message Out," *USA Today*, 29 November 1994, sec. C, p. 2.
12. Rosie Mestel, "I'll Have the Cessna," *In Health* (December/January 1992), 14.
13. "Husband Pleads for Wife Who Ran Him Down," *Chicago Tribune*, 5 January 1995, sec. 1, p. 20.
14. "New Horseradish Variety: Hazardous-Materials-Unit Hot," *Chicago Tribune*, 15 February 1995, sec. 1, p. 10.
15. "China May Sell Laser That Blinds," *Chicago Tribune*, 4 May 1995, sec. 1, p. 24.
16. Mike Harden, "Dictionary's Omissions the Definition of Baffling," *Chicago Tribune*, 23 August 1994, sec. 5, pp. 1, 5.
17. Alan Nelson, *Broken in the Right Place* (Nashville: Thomas Nelson, 1994), 65, 71, 72.

18. Jan Riggenbach, "Midwest Gardening," *Daily Herald*, 8 May 1994.
19. Kathleen Kroll Driscoll, *Rockland (Massachusetts) South Shore News*, as seen in *Reader's Digest* (November 1993), 145.
20. James Coates, "'Good Times' Virus Is Just a Bad On-Line Myth," *Chicago Tribune*, 21 May 1995, sec. 1, pp. 1, 17.
21. Bill Barnhart, "Market Report: In the Heat of Battle, Traders Rule," *Chicago Tribune*, 25 April 1994, sec. 4, p. 1.
22. Don Moser, "Offerings at The Wall," *Smithsonian* (June 1995), 55.
Thomas B. Allen, *Offerings at the Wall* (Atlanta: Turner Publishing, 1995).
23. "Woman's Body Is Found in Kitchen—4 Years after Dying," *Chicago Tribune*, 27 October 1993.
24. "Dead Body Found under Bed in Hotel," *Chicago Tribune*, 13 March 1994, sec. 1, p. 23.
25. Erik Erikson, *Identity: Youth and Crisis* (New York: W.W. Norton, 1968), 17–18.
26. Anne Keegan, "Chicago Speak," *Chicago Tribune*, 24 February 1995, sec. 5, p. 1.
27. Robert Johnson, "Born-Again Surgeon Is at One with God but Not with Peers," *Wall Street Journal*, 6 June 1994, sec. A, p. 1.
28. Jim Long, "Everything Changes," *Campus Life* (October 1994), 30.
29. Lloyd Ogilvie, *Enjoying God* (Dallas: Word, 1989), 21.
30. Mark Memmott, "Economists' Elder Statesman," *USA Today*, 26 September 1994, sec. B, p. 3.
31. Vivian Marino, "In Jewelry, Looks Can Be Deceiving," *Chicago Tribune*, 23 March 1995, sec. 6, p. 3.
32. Rosa Parks, *Quiet Strength* (Grand Rapids: Zondervan, 1995).
33. George de Lama, "Cool Customers," *Chicago Tribune*, 17 May 1994, sec. 5, p. 1.
34. Nelson, *Broken in the Right Place*, 41–42.

35. Steve Jones, "Nichelle Nichols' Bold 'Trek' Following Her Own Star," *USA Today,* 28 November 1994, sec. D, p. 6.

36. John W. Yates, "Overcoming Discouragement," *Preaching Today*, no. 42.

37. "Lawnmower Traveler Spurns Trains and Planes," *Chicago Tribune*, 3 September 1994, sec. 1, p. 4.

38. Reuters, *America Online*, 13 December 1994.

39. William Oscar Johnson, "The Son Finally Rises," *Sports Illustrated* (21 February 1994), 20–28.

40. George O. Wood, "Life's Alternatives," *Pentecostal Evangel* (26 March 1995), 6.

41. Jane E. Brody, "Human Eye Is Reported to Set Clock for the Body," *New York Times*, 5 January 1995, sec. A, p. 8.

42. Johnson, "The Son Finally Rises," 20–28.

43. Per Ola and Emily d'Aulaire, "Now What Are They Doing at That Crazy St. John the Divine?" *Smithsonian* (December 1992), 32.

44. Peter Kendall, "Songbirds Dwindle; Imposters Thrive," *Chicago Tribune*, 1 April 1995, sec. 1, p. 1.

45. Jim Doherty, "For All Who Crave a Horn That Thrills, This Bud's for You," *Smithsonian* (September 1994), 96.

46. Mickey Mantle with Jill Lieber, "Time in a Bottle," *Sports Illustrated* (18 April 1994), 66–77.

47. "Author Penick Dies at 90," *Chicago Tribune*, 4 April 1995, sec. 4, p. 2.

48. "Uh, Oh. Pull Over—and Get a Thank-You," *Chicago Tribune,* 13 June 1993.

49. Reuters, *America Online,* 20 January 1995.

50. Reuters, *America Online*, 22 November 1994.

51. Graham R. Hodges, "The Lesson of the Cocklebur," *Leadership* (fall 1988), 129.

52. "Captain Remembers Nuclear Horror on Soviet Submarine," *Chicago Tribune*, 20 August 1993, sec. 1, p. 4.

53. Mike Lupica, "Amazing Grace," *Esquire* (February 1995).

54. "Biz Tips: Admit to Screwups?" *Chicago Tribune*, 17 April 1995, sec. 4, p. 3.

55. Ann Landers, "Freak Accidents Have Motorists Tongue-tied," *Chicago Tribune*, 24 August 1994, sec. 5, p. 3.

56. Larry Burkett, *Business by the Book* (Nashville: Nelson, 1990), 9–11.

57. "Summer Swan Song," *Life* (October 1993), 12–13.

58. Philip Yancey, "What Surprised Jesus," *Christianity Today* (12 September 1994) 88.

59. "Penny for Your Thoughts, Dear Ex-Wife," *Chicago Tribune* online.

60. Jan Senn, "Carol Kent on Keeping Confident," *Today's Christian Woman* (January/February 1995), 68.

61. Matthew Mak, "Getting Over It: Fearful Drivers Get Help across Bridges," *USA Today*, 5 August 1992, sec. A, p. 6.

62. "Fatal Overreaction," *Time* (14 August 1989), 33.

63. Cindy Schreuder, "Science of the Seasons: Spring, the Miracle of Renewal," *Chicago Tribune*, 24 May 1995, sec. 1, p. 1.

64. Douglas H. Chadwick, "On the Edge of Earth and Sky," *National Geographic* (April 1995), 116.

65. Gordon MacDonald, *Restoring Your Spiritual Passion* (Nashville: Oliver-Nelson, 1986), 104–5.

66. Charles Swindoll, *The Grace Awakening* (Dallas: Word, 1990), 47–48.

67. "French Woman Marks 120th—Yes—Birthday," *Chicago Tribune*, 22 February 1995, sec. 1, p. 9.

68. Bill and Lynne Hybels, *Honest to God* (Grand Rapids: Zondervan, 1990), 39.

69. "Love Pays Off Big for Harvard Law School," *Chicago Tribune,* 3 October 1994, sec. 1, p. 14.

70. Stu Weber, "What It Takes to Reach Men," *Leadership* (fall 1994), 128.

71. Carrie Dowling, "'The Baby's Here'—At 30,000 Feet," *USA Today,* 28 November 1994, sec. A, p. 3.

72. "The Shirt off My Back," *USA Today,* 20 May 1994.

73. Robert E. Wells, *Is a Blue Whale the Biggest Thing There Is?* (Morton Grove, Ill.: Albert Whitman & Company, 1993).

74. "Father Wants Defector Back from Korea," *Chicago Tribune*, 20 September 1982, sec. 1, p. 4.

75. Ramona Cramer Tucker, "Bodie Thoene: True Grit," *Today's Christian Woman* (September/October 1994), 61.

76. "Scorecard," *Sports Illustrated* (27 June 1988), 9.

77. Frank W. Mann Jr., *Robins Reader*, as seen in *Reader's Digest* (May 1995), 209–10.

78. Martha Moore, "Shoe Firm Sets Pace, Wins Awards," *USA Today*, 24 June 1994, sec. B, pp. 1–2.

79. Tony Campolo, *World Vision* (October/November 1988).

81. Spencer Reiss and Nina Archer Biddle, "The Strep-A Scare," *Newsweek* (20 June 1994), 32–33.

82. "It's a Frozen Tower of Pisa," *Chicago Tribune*, 19 April 1995, sec. 1, p. 3.

83. Paul Francisco, "Lite Fare," *The Christian Reader* (March/April 1993), 38.

84. "14 Hours And 9 Miles Later, Answer Is Still No," *Chicago Tribune* online, 28 July 1994.

85. William Langewiesche, "The Turn," *Atlantic Monthly* (December 1993), 115–22.

86. Swindoll, *The Grace Awakening*, 9.

87. Marya Smith, "First Person: Deposition Reader," *Chicago Tribune Magazine* (13 June 1993), 33.

88. Barbara Kantrowitz et al., "The Fugitive," *Time* (27 September 1993), 54–60.

89. Jon Van, "'Jackhammer' Used in Clearing Arteries," *Chicago Tribune*, 10 November 1993, sec. 1, p. 7.

90. "Secretive Censor Defacing Books," *Chicago Tribune*, 22 May 1994, sec. 1, p. 8.

91. Ken Jones, *When You're All Out of Noodles* (Nashville: Thomas Nelson, 1993).

92. Dave Dravecky with Ken Gire, *When You Can't Come Back* (Grand Rapids: Zondervan, 1992).

93. Max Lucado, *Six Hours One Friday* (Sisters, Ore.: Multnomah, 1989), 43–44.

94. John von Rhein, "Alarms Go Off with CSO Ending Its Centenary Season," *Chicago Tribune*, 20 October 1991, sec. 5, p. 5.

95. Lisa Belcher-Hamilton, "The Gospel According to Fred: A Visit with Mr. Rogers," *The Christian Century* (13 April 1994), 382.

96. Charles Swindoll, *Flying Closer to the Flame* (Dallas: Word, 1993), 71–73.

97. Ogilvie, *Enjoying God,* 50.

98. Paul Quinnett, *Pavlov's Trout* (Keokee), as seen in *Reader's Digest* (May 1995), 210.

100. David Neff, "Why Hope Is a Virtue," *Christianity Today* (3 April 1995), 24.

101. Ronald Pinkerton, *Guideposts* (September 1988).

102. James W. Arnold, *St. Anthony Messenger,* as seen in *Reader's Digest* (April 1995), 25.

103. "Judges Deflate Texas Steer's Championship," *Chicago Tribune,* 7 June 1992, sec. 1, p. 24.

104. *Christianity Today* (25 April 1994), 44.

105. Nancy V. Raine, "Returns of the Day," *New York Times Magazine* (2 October 1994), 34.

106. *New England Journal of Medicine* (2 March 1995), 614.

107. "Even Blindfolded, Moms Show Touch for Newborns," *Chicago Tribune.*

108. Philip Hersh, "Solid Gold," *Chicago Tribune*, 9 November 1994, sec. 5, p. 1.

Dave Kindred, "What Was Meant to Be," *Sporting News* (28 February 1994), 10–11.

109. Tom Friend, "This Time, Dad Can't Stop Joe from Quitting," *Chicago Tribune*, 19 April 1995, sec. 4, p. 3.

110. "Supreme Court Turns Deaf Ear to 1,600 Appeals," *Chicago Tribune*, 4 October 1994, sec. 1, p. 3.

111. "Why We Pray," *Life* (March 1994), 59.

112. Charles Krauthammer, "Slippery When Upset," *Chicago Tribune*, 5 May 1995, sec. 1, p. 21.

113. Ron Grossman, "The Big Fellow," *Chicago Tribune*, 24 August 1994, sec. 5, pp. 1–2.

114. "In California City, Acts of Kindness Are Becoming Contagious," *Chicago Tribune*, 29 October 1993.

115. Phillip Keller, *Pleasures Forevermore* (Eugene, Ore.: Harvest House, 1992), 47–49.

116. Jon Van, "Study Finds Doctors Respond Well to Sweet Treatment," *Chicago Tribune*, 22 February 1995, sec. 1, p. 4.

117. James Coates, "Orbiting On-line: The Evolution of the Internet," *Chicago Tribune*, 26 March 1995, sec. 7, p. 4.

118. "Mississippi Senate Votes to Ban Slavery," *Chicago Tribune*, 17 February 1995, sec. 1, p. 11.

119. Philip Yancey, "As Casey Stengel Said . . ." *Christianity Today*.

120. Gary Fields, "Oil-spill Research Ship Hits Fragile Reef, Leaks Fuel," *USA Today*, 12–14 August 1994, sec. A, p. 1.

121. Scott Turow, *Presumed Innocent* (New York: Farrar, Straus, and Giroux, 1987), 3.

122. Leith Anderson, "The Trouble with Legalism," *Moody* (October 1994), 15.

123. Robert Frank, "As UPS Tries to Deliver More to Its Customers, Labor Problems Grow," *Wall Street Journal*, 23 May 1994, sec. A, p. 1.

124. Lynn Austin, "Satan's Tackle Box," *The Christian Reader* (July/August 1994), 55–56. Abridged from *Moody*.

125. "French Woman Marks 120th—Yes—Birthday," *Chicago Tribune*, 22 February 1995, sec. 1, p. 9.

126. As abridged in *The Christian Reader* (May/June 1995), 34.

127. Gordon Wilson, "When Love Meets a Brick Wall," *World Vision* (June/July 1994), 12–13.

128. Bruce Thielemann, "Legions of the Unjazzed," *Preaching Today*, no. 36.

129. Paul Pearsall, *The Ten Laws of Lasting Love* (New York: Simon & Schuster, 1993), as seen in *Reader's Digest* (March 1995), 148–49.

130. Philip Yancey, "The Riddle of Bill Clinton's Faith," *Christianity Today* (25 April 1994), 29.

Chuck Colson, "How to Confront a President," *Christianity Today* (25 April 1994), 64.

131. Stephen Franklin, "Lessons from a Labor-Management War," *Chicago Tribune*, 15 May 1994, sec. 7, p. 1.

132. Ogilvie, *Enjoying God*, 19–20.

133. "A Secret Song," *Time* (13 February 1989), 41.

134. "Bride Gives Groom a Lifesaver in Form of a Transplanted Kidney," *Chicago Tribune*, 10 November 1994, sec. 1, p. 6.

"Bride-to-be Promises Hand, Heart—and Kidney to Fiancé," *Chicago Tribune*, 10 October 1994, sec. 1, p. 2.

135. James Dobson, *Focus on the Family Newsletter* (February 1995).

137. Tom Junod, "Arms and the Man," *Sports Illustrated* (14 June 1993), 72, 74.

138. Ron Kotulak and Jon Van, "Flying Jets with Brain Power," *Chicago Tribune*, 12 February 1995, sec. 5, p. 3.

139. Reuters, "Chinese Doctors Take Pin from Brain after 40 Years," *America Online*, 29 October 1994.

140. Phyllis Berman, "Harry's a Great Storyteller," *Forbes* (27 February 1995), 116.

141. Jim Doherty, "For All Who Crave a Horn That Thrills, This Bud's for You," *Smithsonian* (September 1994), 102.

142. "Self-taught Chef Has Star Quality," *Chicago Tribune*, 6 March 1995, sec. 1, p. 2.

143. "Health Deduction for Self-Employed OKd," *Chicago Tribune*, 4 April 1995, sec. 1, p. 3.

144. Ron Kotulak and Jon Van, "A Cliché Proven," *Chicago Tribune*, 15 August 1993, sec. 5, p. 4.

145. Howard Witt, "Armenia Turns to Time Bomb for Fuel," *Chicago Tribune*, 22 November 1993, sec. 1, p. 1.

146. Porter B. Williamson, *General Patton's Principles for Life and Leadership* (Tucson: Management & Systems Consultants, Inc., 1988).

147. "Crash Probe Focuses on Ice Buildup," *Chicago Tribune*, 25 March 1992.

148. Elizabeth Mittelstaedt, "Afterwords," *Today's Christian Woman* (January/February 1995), 72.

149. Alan Mairson, "America's Beekeepers," *National Geographic* (May 1993), 82–83.

150. Nelson, *Broken in the Right Place,* 43.

151. "Half of Sexually Active Teens Tell Survey: Wish I'd Waited," *Chicago Tribune,* 18 May 1994.

152. Bob Greene, "I Know I Have at Least One Fan," *Chicago Tribune,* 15 August 1993, sec. 5, p. 1.

153. LeAnn Spencer, "Botanic Garden Viewing Century Plant's Growth as the Stalk of the Town," *Chicago Tribune,* 11 April 1995, sec. 1, p. 1.

154. "Got a Minute? That's All an Episode Takes," *Chicago Tribune,* 18 August 1994, sec. 1, p. 19.

156. Jorge Casuso, "Epic in the Making," *Chicago Tribune,* 5 December 1991, sec. 5, p. 1.

157. "New Beatles Lyrics? Not Eggzactly," *Chicago Tribune,* 10 March 1995, sec. 1, p. 2.

158. Dan Jansen, *Full Circle* (New York: Villard Books, 1994).

159. "Satellite 'Skips' down to Earth," *Chicago Tribune,* 29 October 1993, sec. 1, p. 19.

160. Rita Rubin, "Cholesterol, Round 2," *U.S. News & World Report* (28 June 1993), 61.

161. Gene Sloan, "Arizona Says People Step One Toad over the Line," *USA Today,* 4 August 1994, sec. A, p. 1.

162. "Ordinary Heroes," *The Christian Reader* (January/February 1993), 82.

163. Yancey, "What Surprised Jesus," 88.

164. Blair Walker, "Laws Serve Lemon-Aid to Car Buyers," *USA Today,* 23 May 1994.

165. "$900-million Venus Probe Plunges to Its End," *Chicago Tribune,* 13 October 1994, sec. 1, p. 27.

166. Harold Kushner, *Who Needs God* (New York: Summit, 1989).

167. J. K. Gressett, "Take Courage," *Pentecostal Evangel* (30 April 1989), 6.

168. John Fischer, *Contemporary Christian Music* (August 1992).

169. Hyatt Moore, "Praying a Bible into Existence," *The Christian Reader* (January/February 1993), 46.

170. James Overstreet, "When E-mail Turns to J(unk)-Mail," *USA Today,* 26 September 1994, sec. B, p. 7.

171. Haddon Robinson, "The Disciple's Prayer," *Preaching Today,* no. 117.

172. Charles Colson, "The Blind Leading the Blind," *BreakPoint,* (April 1994).

173. Ken O'Brien, "Would You Trade?" *Chicago Tribune,* 15 May 1994, sec. 18, pp. 1, 4.

174. "Waitress Takes Tip That's Worth Millions," *Chicago Tribune,* 4 April 1984, sec. 1, p. 6.

175. Susan Hazen-Hammond, "'Horny Toads' Enjoy a Special Place in Western Hearts," *Smithsonian* (December 1994), 90.

176. "Sign of the Times," *Chicago Tribune,* 8 October 1993.

177. "From Film to Art," *USA Today,* 28 November 1994, sec. D, p. 1.

178. James Dobson, *When God Doesn't Make Sense* (Wheaton: Tyndale House, 1994).

179. John Robb and Brenda Spoelstra, "A Miracle in Moscow," *World Vision* (August/September 1991), 13.

180. Bryan Wilkerson, "A Purpose Runs through It," *Preaching Today,* no. 133.

181. Corrie ten Boom, *The Hiding Place* (Grand Rapids: Chosen, 1988).

182. Melissa Isaacson, "Fan Hits 1 in Million—and Bulls Win, Too," *Chicago Tribune,* 15 April 1993, sec. 4, p. 1.

Kent McDill, "Shot Heard 'Round the World," *Suburban Chicago Daily Herald,* 15 April 1993, sec. 3, p. 5.

183. "Ex-Cornell Militant Names Prize after Old Foe," *Chicago Tribune,* 5 May 1995, sec. 1, p. 12.

184. Jancee Dunn, *Rolling Stone* (30 June 1994), 35.

185. William Willimon, "The Writing on the Wall," *Preaching Today,* no. 129.

186. "Injured Woodsman Pinned under Tree, Amputates Leg," *Chicago Tribune,* 22 July 1993, sec. 1, p. 9.

Pam Lambert and Tom Nugent, *People* (9 August 1993), 42.

187. David Margolick, "Best O.J. Reporting from—Would You Believe—The National Enquirer?" *Chicago Tribune Online,* 27 October 1994.

188. John H. Timmerman, "Black Gold: Nurturing the Heart," *Moody* (September 1994), 14.

189. "Pyrotechnician Says Farewell by Rocket's Red Glare," *Chicago Tribune*, 14 August 1994, sec. 1, p. 6.

190. Ron Kotulak and Jon Van, "Discoveries: Laser Provides Unexpected Sight," *Chicago Tribune*, 30 April 1995, sec. 5, p. 5.

191. Kevin Maney, "Sony's Legend Stepping Down," *USA Today*, 28 November 1994, sec. B, p. 2.

192. Bob Greene, "A Young Athlete's Greatest Move," *Chicago Tribune*, 18 December 1994, Tempo section, p. 1.

Kevin Dale Miller, "Ordinary Heroes," *The Christian Reader* (May/June 1995), 35.

193. Gordon MacDonald, *Ordering Your Private World* (Nashville: Oliver-Nelson, 1985), 106–7.

194. MacDonald, *Restoring Your Spiritual Passion,* 51–52.

195. Ann Landers, "This Surgeon Was Definitely Out to Lunch," *Chicago Tribune*, 12 February 1995, sec. 5, p. 3.

196. "'Mystery Fare' Leaves Some Sad, Some Glad," *Chicago Tribune*, 28 August 1994, sec. 1, p. 4.

197. Phillip Fiorini, "Computer Programming Pioneer Kildall Dies at 52," *USA Today*, 14 July 1994, sec. B, p. 2.

198. Ted Gregory, "The Informer," *Chicago Tribune*, 5 May 1995, sec. 5, p. 1.

199. William Langewiesche, "The Turn," *Atlantic Monthly* (December 1993), 115–22.

200. Michael Parfit, "And What Words Shall Describe the Mississippi, Great Father of Rivers?" *Smithsonian* (February 1993), 36.

201. Cheryl Lavin, "Fast Track," *Chicago Tribune Magazine* (13 June 1993), 10.

202. Isak Dinesen, *Out of Africa* (New York: Ingram, 1988).

203. Janice Castro, "When the Chips Are Down," *Time* (26 December 1994), 126.

204. "660-pound Man Dies after Eating Piglet," *Chicago Tribune*, 17 December 1993.

205. "Stuck in Reverse, Driverless Car Snarls Traffic for 2 Hours," *Chicago Tribune*, 10 November 1994, sec. 1, p. 9.

206. "State Trooper Guilty of Planting Bombs," *New York Times*, 6 January 1995, sec. A, p. 12.

207. "Praise for Indian Dung," *Chicago Tribune*, 8 September 1994, sec. 1, p. 4.

208. Sue Allison Massimiano and Claudia Glenn Dowling, "The Demobilization of Colin Powell," *Life* (July 1993), 43.

209. Harvey Mackay, "Avoid Contagious Business Flaw," *Chicago Tribune*, 6 December 1993, sec. 4, p. 10.

210. Lawrence Van Gelder, "Victor Riesel, 81, Columnist Blinded by Acid Attack, Dies," *New York Times*, 5 January 1995, sec. A, p. 17.

211. Gene B. Williams, *All Thumbs Guide to VCRs* (Blue Ridge Summit, Pa.: Tab Books, 1993), 1.

212. Tom Cunneff, "The Great White's Ways," *Sports Illustrated* (15 May 1995), 8.

213. "Last Stores of Smallpox Virus Doomed," *Chicago Tribune*, 10 September 1994, sec. 1, p. 16.

Donald A. Henderson, "Smallpox," *The World Book Encyclopedia* (1985).

214. Jacquelyn Heard and William Recktenwald, "Teachers Union Springs to the Defense of Exonerated Substitute," *Chicago Tribune*, 18 May 1994, sec. 2, p. 5.

Chicago Tribune Magazine (1 January 1995), 16.

215. Howard Witt, "Art's Miniature Man," *Chicago Tribune,* 1 August 1993, sec. 5, p. 1.

216. John Killinger, "Finding God in a Busy World," *Preaching Today,* no. 132.

217. Ogilvie, *Enjoying God*, 53–54.

218. Robert Sullivan, *Life* (October 1993), 10.

219. Gary Marx, "Space Race," *Chicago Tribune*, 15 August 1993, sec. 5, pp. 1, 6.

220. Rudolph Chelminski, "Any Way You Slice It, a Poilane Loaf Is Real French Bread," *Smithsonian* (January 1995), 54, 56.

221. Hybels, *Honest to God*, 26–27.

222. Michael A. Lev, "Injured Violinist Has a Special Kind of Pluck," *Chicago Tribune*, 22 March 1995, sec. 1, p. 1.

223. John Wimber, "John Wimber Calls It Power Evangelism," *Charisma* (September 1985), 38.

224. "You Can Tell It's a Mink by Its Tiny Periscope," *Chicago Tribune*, 9 February 1995, sec. 1, p. 23.

225. Robert Duran, *The Christian Reader* (January/February 1993), 47.

226. "MCI Worker Is Charged in Huge Phone-card Theft," *Chicago Tribune*, 4 October 1994.

227. Nelson, *Broken in the Right Place*, 84–85.

228. Reuters, "Man Shoots Self Four Times in Head but Lives," *America Online*, 1 November 1994.

229. Paul Sitter, "Worst in a Decade," *The Parachutist* (July 1994), 21.

230. "Pearl Jam Soars" and "Quotables," *Chicago Tribune*, 30 October 1993, sec. 1, pp. 21–22.

231. Stevenson Swanson, "From Death, Life," *Chicago Tribune*, 23 April 1995, sec. 5, pp. 1, 6.

232. Bob Greene, "I Know I Have at Least One Fan," *Chicago Tribune*, 15 August 1993, sec. 5, p. 1.

233. "Bone-bonding Compound Hastens Fracture Repair," *Chicago Tribune*, 24 March 1995, sec. 1, p. 15.

234. Charles Stanley, *The Wonderful Spirit Filled Life* (Nashville: Thomas Nelson, 1992), 48–49.

235. "There Goes the Neighborhood," *Life* (November 1993), 24.

236. "Mattress Too Lumpy for Comfort— She Finds a Bomb under It," *Chicago Tribune*, 16 April 1983, sec. 1, p. 5.

237. Michael Lipske, "Forget Hollywood: These Bloodthirsty Beauties Are for Real," *Smithsonian* (December 1992), 49–59.

238. Lynn Austin, "Satan's Tackle Box," *The Christian Reader* (July/August 1994), 55–56. Abridged from *Moody*.

239. Joni Eareckson Tada, *Secret Strength* (Portland: Multnomah Press, 1988), 29–30.

240. "Drinking the Sky," *Life* (November 1993), 80–84.

241. *Newsweek* (20 June 1994).

242. Alan P. Xenakis, *Why Doesn't My Funny Bone Make Me Laugh?* (New York: Villard, 1993).

243. "'Trapped' Yuppie Tells Why He Dropped Out," *Chicago Tribune*, 5 February 1989, sec. 1, p. 10.

244. Sandra Blakeslee, "A Fiery Volcano in Colombia Is Said to Be Spewing Gold," *New York Times*, 28 October 1994, sec. 1, p. 1.

245. Susan Wloszczyna, "Actor-director Alchemy Brings Out the Best in Both," *USA Today*, 1 August 1994, sec. D, p. 4.

246. Harold Myra, *Living by God's Surprises* (Dallas: Word, 1988), 84.

247. Reuters, "This Just In," *America Online*, 11 December 1994.

248. Joe Morgenstern, "The Fifty-Nine-Story Crisis," *New Yorker* (29 May 1995), 47.

249. Jorge Casuso, "Epic in the Making," *Chicago Tribune*, 5 December 1991, sec. 5, p. 1.

250. "Final Salute for Cleared 'Deserter,'" *Chicago Tribune*, 2 February 1983.

251. "Unique Lens Explains Chameleons' Super-vision," *Chicago Tribune*, 23 February 1995, sec. 1, p. 16.

252. James O'Shea, "Report Cites Mistakes by Ship, Plane," *Chicago Tribune*, 14 June 1987, sec. 1, p. 1.

253. Morgenstern, "The Fifty-Nine-Story Crisis," 45–53.

254. John Waggoner, "Templeton Celebrates, Looks to Future," *USA Today*, 1 August 1994, sec. B, p. 4.

255. Anita Manning, "Anatomy of a Research Tool," *USA Today*, 29 November 1994, sec. D, p. 1.

256. "'Serial Eater' Dines in High Style on His Way to Slammer," *Chicago Tribune*, 22 May 1994, sec. 1, p. 21.

257. "Worker Chasing Hat Killed on Tollway," *Chicago Tribune*, 4 March 1995, sec. 1, p. 5.

258. Bill Moyers, *A World of Ideas* (New York: Doubleday, 1989).

259. William R. Newcott, "Lightning," *National Geographic* (July 1993), 83–103.

260. Kate Eaton, "All Aboard!" *Chicago Tribune*, 4 September 1994, sec. 17, pp. 1, 5.

Subject Index

reaping, 51, 52, 113, 212
receiving Christ, 29, 182, 185
reconciliation, 183
redemption, 184
refreshment, 240
regret, 8, 46
relationships, 48
remembrance, 22
repentance, 24, 63, 78, 89, 110, 182, 185, 186, 223, 227
reputation, 187, 206, 214, 250, 253
resentment, 65, 72
respect, 53, 195
responsibility, 193, 256
rest, 188
restoration, 211
resurrection, 33, 189
revelation, 190
revenge, 7
reverence, 166, 195
revival, 63
rewards, 21, 191
righteousness, 32, 85, 192
risk, 2, 57, 128, 191
roots, 180
routine, 193
rulers, 82
rules, 122

Sabbath, 188, 194
sacred, 195
sacrifice, 34, 35, 37, 63, 69, 84, 128, 130, 134, 249
safety, 176
salvation, 1, 5, 16, 79, 83, 84, 85, 110, 140, 182, 184, 196, 197, 207, 247
Satan, 15, 198, 212, 218, 224, 236, 237
saving, 254
science, 33
Scripture, 101, 199
second coming, 200, 201, 202, 252
secrets, 133, 203, 223
security, 97
seeds, 51

self-centeredness, 17
self-control, 8, 138, 204, 205, 236, 242
self-deception, 111
self-discipline, 193
self-esteem, 208
self-image, 230
selfish ambition, 206
selfishness, 35
self-reliance, 106, 247
self-respect, 230
self-righteousness, 207
self-sufficiency, 97
self-worth, 208
servanthood, 209
service, 35, 57, 260
sex, 151, 181
sexual sin, 253
shame, 88, 133, 210
sharing, 76
shepherding, 4
significance, 112, 131, 230
silence, 91
sin, 25, 26, 55, 66, 80, 145, 184, 186, 211, 212, 213, 237
sinful nature, 226
slander, 214, 250
sloth, 42
small things, 215
solitude, 91, 216
sovereignty of God, 67, 154, 177, 179, 180, 215, 227
sowing, 51, 52, 113, 212
spiritual discernment, 91, 141, 217, 218, 236, 251
spiritual disciplines, 39, 91, 216, 219, 220, 221
spiritual gifts, 71, 140, 190, 222, 223
spirituality, 14, 123, 219
spiritual sickness, 20
spiritual warfare, 15, 224, 225
sports, 158
sportsmanship, 192
stability, 248
status, 102
stealing, 218, 226, 256
stinginess, 59

strength, 68, 137
stress, 188, 216, 243, 244
struggle, 184
stubbornness, 227, 228
study, 142
stumbling, 229
submission, 82, 159
success, 157, 221, 230, 251, 254
suffering, 21, 148, 150, 154, 175, 231, 239
suicide, 148, 228
support, 232, 233
surprise, 159
surrender, 234
sympathy, 105

taxes, 82
teachability, 6, 47
teachers, 120
teaching, 142
teamwork, 71
technique, 141
teenagers, 126, 151, 192
television, 49
temper, 8, 175
temporal, 21, 92, 94, 235, 257
temptation, 2, 149, 198, 211, 229, 236, 237, 238, 239, 242
Ten Commandments, 104, 112, 226
testing, 17, 19
thanks, 48, 116
thanksgiving, 58, 77, 160, 167, 240, 241
thirst, 240
thoughts, 12, 49, 65, 138, 139, 242
time, 154, 173
tongue, 81
tragedy, 147, 181
training, 141
trapped, 243
trauma, 222
trials, 17, 99, 101, 149, 167, 181, 216, 231, 244, 248
trouble, 145, 248

Scripture Index

About the Author

Craig Brian Larson serves as contributing editor of *Leadership Journal* and for four years edited the magazine's "To Illustrate" column. He pastors in Chicago.